The Grand National

Also by Vian Smith

ADULT FICTION

Question Mark
Press Gang
Genesis Down
The First Thunder
The Wind Blows Free

JUNIOR FICTION

Martin Rides the Moor
King Sam
The Horses of Petrock
Come Down the Mountain
The Lord Mayor's Show
Green Heart

NON-FICTION

A Horse Called Freddie
Point-to-Point
Portrait of Dartmoor

TELEVISION PLAYS

The First Thunder
Giants on Saturday

VIAN SMITH

THE GRAND NATIONAL

A history of the world's greatest steeplechase

STANLEY PAUL | LONDON

STANLEY PAUL & CO LTD
178–202 Great Portland Street, London W1

AN IMPRINT OF THE HUTCHINSON GROUP

London Melbourne Sydney
Auckland Bombay Toronto
Johannesburg New York

★

First published 1969

This book has been set in Plantin, printed in Great Britain on Antique Wove paper by Anchor Press, and bound by Wm. Brendon, both of Tiptree, Essex

09 095630 3

For Roma and Sebastian

Illustrations

Between pages 168 and 169

Troytown, the winner of 1920
The first fence in 1965
Bogskar leads MacMoffat over the last in 1940
Kapeno leads at the Chair in 1966
Royal Tan gets home from Tudor Line in 1954

I

The time, 9.30. The place, Exchange Station, Liverpool. The destination, Aintree. It's Grand National morning and the faithful are arriving. They are Scots and Welsh; they're the singing half of Ireland. They've come through the night from north and south, east and west and the railway faces couldn't give a damn.

'First on the right,' a uniform says, meaning its right, which is our left. There's confusion, none knowing which platform or which train until a woman calls from a carriage window and everyone goes left.

These women know all about Grand National day. They've been going to Aintree since the year Prince Regent almost won. They're not going to watch. They're going to work; serious work behind bars, flipping metal caps from light ales and handing us wet change. Meanwhile they smoke filter tips and slip down their head-scarves and talk about their rights.

The train rattles towards industrial chimneys and small houses and washing on the line. When it darts through a cutting the houses on either side seem high, the windows as far away as the port-holes of a ship when you're standing on the quay. Where there are no houses, only spaces like memories of war, there is grass. The grass is long and pale. It weeps down the embankments, mourning the mugs who will lose today.

Aintree is 'Sefton country'. Until 1949 the Earls of Sefton

were its landlords. The pub on the corner is the Sefton Arms and men stand outside it, watching traffic pass towards Walton. They are waiting for something English and anti-Irish called opening time. It's here you'll find Irish boasts before the race and Irish explanations after it.

Queues are forming at the racecourse gates. Coaches arrive with empties already in the crates. 'Kiss me' hats wave from the windows, suggesting that there's not much work being done in Chorley and Bolton today. Cars thicken on the Ormskirk road. A boy watches a policeman and the policeman watches the boy. The police will need to be vigilant today. Getting in for nothing is part of the Aintree 'game'.

Traffic wardens patrol the Melling Road. This is the road which millions know who have never seen it. It's a long line of semi-detached houses which seem remote from National day. Women are talking over the fence. They aren't talking about horses or what the newspapers are tipping. They're talking about babies and what their husbands told the foreman. They glance to passing pedestrians with a kind of hostility. They are proud of the race. They will show resentment if you suggest it might be transferred from Liverpool or could survive elsewhere. But their privacy is being touched. They want to live quietly yet to have the race as well.

Today their road ceases to be only a road and becomes involved with horses and television and commentators gabbling into microphones. It crosses the circuit in two places and eight workmen wait near Seeds Lane Cottages to cover tarmac with ashes. They lean on their shovels to chat about the old days; when the Grand National was held on a Friday to keep the workers out. Of course the workers came. They came in their thousands. But Grand National week was also a time for entertaining at country houses in Cheshire and Lancashire and North Wales. It seemed to be the one week in the year when the aristocratic South considered Liverpool socially permissible.

Then something happened. The shovel-men will tell you it was partly the war, partly the Cheltenham Gold Cup, but chiefly it was television. The 'telly' changed it all because you don't need to come now. You can sit at home and see more in greater comfort for far less.

'Why are you here?' the workmen ask.

We're here on a sentimental journey, for this Grand National, like others in recent years, might be the last. Because of this we're prepared to put up with the inconvenience inherent in attendance, even to suffer those notices. No change. No cameras. No pass-outs. 'No' is the most depressing word in the language and must be a poor welcome for those who have made long journeys.

One of the traditions of Grand National morning is to walk the course. It is to satisfy public demand that the programme announces: 'Owing to complaints received by the Management that, apart from County Stand Badge holders, there are no facilities for the public to view Becher's, Canal Turn, Valentines, etc., it is pointed out that the following procedure should be adopted . . .'

A loudspeaker tinkles polite piano music as we begin to walk. It's like walking into history, for this is where it happened all the way back to Lottery and Jim Mason, who wore white gloves, to hotel proprietor Lynn, who was sure he'd make a fortune.

The grass is closely knit and has a lilt like celebration. It seems to be celebrating the weather, for Aintree weather is usually mist or rain or snow or sleet, even the lot simultaneously. But today there's a sun up there, knocking to come through. The colours are brightest where the sun is pointing, and the colours at Aintree are red and green and white and yellow.

Most of the fences are generously sloped at the base and their tops are rounded like teenage shoulders. They are of two kinds. Open ditches are of spruce, packed in layers like the skins of an onion. Other fences are of green gorse. It seems a misnomer to call them 'thorn', but that is the official description.

The Chair is the most formidable fence on the stands side. It is an open ditch. The edge of the ditch is a white line, like the edge of a pavement during the wartime black-out. The spruce has a base of heavy sleepers. Beside it is the iron chair from which it gets its name.

It's on the far side of the course that you find the famous fences; each with a name and a past and a kind of personality. The Canal Turn has a long, blind wing to conceal the sharp left-hand turn to approaching horses. There are concrete tiers beside it and the first spectators have arrived; some standing, as conspicuous as penguins on an ice-flow, one family sitting around their transistor while Mother opens the vacuum flask and Father lifts the top flap of a sandwich, then groans because it's cheese.

Anchor Bridge is formidable. So is Valentine's, served by the stream which goes on to Becher's. Near Valentine's the iron struts of the rails are padded with yellow foam rubber.

The twenty-third fence has no name, yet its history of disaster is recent. It was here that the race of 1967 became a farce, so many horses becoming involved in confusion that a blinkered nonentity, derisively dismissed in the morning papers, got away to win. A cold figure with earphones like ear-muffs stands by it, waiting to record what happens this year.

So we come to Becher's, the most famous fence in the world. The brook is on the touch-down side. It trundles from a hole on one side to a grill on the other and seems a meagre thing to be so famous. There are 'B' flags at either end, showing Americans that this is it; the fence which Battleship survived in 1938 and which couldn't bring down Jay Trump in 1965. The American response to the biggest anything is to photograph it, but you'll remember the notices at the entrance.

Only professional cameras are allowed and television cameras are there, ready to relay the first and second circuits. To ride over Becher's for the first time is supposed to be like flying or taking your last toe from the bottom if you're a coward swimmer. It's supposed to be something you worry about in anticipation and remember for ever more. But there's a story about professional R. Barnes who rode veteran Wyndburgh to near victory. After the race, when asked his opinion of Becher's, Barnes replied, 'Which one was that?' and earned his place in Aintree folklore.

Flags of many nations line the embankment near the railway.

They hang limply beneath clouds suddenly low enough to touch. It's here, a world removed from the stands and paddock and the bowler hats with their county badges, that you feel closest to the past. It's easy to see the ghosts. They come out of the ground like soldiers rising from the Somme. It's easy to hear the drumming, to hear the drumming quicken, to look leftwards and see the horses coming. They come with battle in their drumming and the first of them isn't Lottery, although in some records he is considered to be the first. The first is The Duke, owned by Mr. Sirdefield and ridden by Mr. Potts. He won in 1837 and that's where Grand National history begins.

2

The year: 1837
Number of runners: Four
Winner: The Duke (Mr. H. Potts—12 st)

The background to this race was a storm of controversy. On one side were Liverpool enthusiasts, sure that steeplechasing could be successfully promoted provided meetings were carefully organised. They pointed to the example which Tom Coleman had set in far-off St. Albans.

Tom was proprietor of the Turf Hotel. He had promoted flat races. In 1830 he introduced steeplechasing, each year improving the organisation so that by 1834 the St. Albans race from Hartlington church to the obelisk in Wrest Park and back was among the big events of the year.

Other towns in the South and Wales were trying to establish local meetings. There was even a March meeting at nearby Blackburn.

It would have been remarkable if Liverpool had not followed the trend. There had been races over four miles at Crosby in 1576. These were the Ascension Day races, revived in the eighteenth century but abandoned for lack of support in 1786. In 1827 landowner John Formby introduced meetings on agricultural land at Maghull and shortly afterwards William Lynn, of the Waterloo Hotel, established a rival meeting at Aintree.

He leased land from the Sefton family and built a grandstand. On July 7th, 1829, the history of Aintree as a racecourse began.

The early races were flat races. Lynn did not experiment with steeplechasing until 1836, when he introduced a race of four miles and twenty fences, plus two hurdles in the straight. It was confined to 'gentlemen' and each horse carried twelve stone. There were ten runners. The winner was The Duke, ridden by Captain Becher.

The response confirmed the popularity of steeplechasing as a spectacle. An observer remarked with surprise that a high proportion of those present seemed to be 'of the middle class'. Other observers were surprised by the enthusiasm, for steeplechasing was not new. There had been 'steeple to steeple' races for more than a hundred years; often the result of challenges offered by one rider to another and called 'matches' when confined to two contestants. But these had been private affairs, organised by and on behalf of participants. No concessions had been made to those who wished to watch. Spectators had needed to be mounted in order to follow events or had needed to anticipate what route the riders would take if they were to see anything.

Moreover, those who had seen the start had not seen the finish. Early races had been straight gallops from one point to another, four or five miles away. The secret of Coleman's success at St. Albans was his insistence that the obelisk at Wrest Park should be a turning-point, so that spectators could gather at the start with the assurance of seeing the finish.

Lynn learned from Coleman. The Aintree course was so designed that the race began and ended near the stands. This meant that spectators on the perimeter or in the centre of the course could take an intelligent and enthusiastic interest. They might still not know the names of horses or riders, for race-cards and number-boards had not been introduced and would have meant little to those who couldn't read, but they were involved in the race and enjoyed the novelty.

Lynn must have thought his fortune made. In 1837 he became more ambitious. The town authority gave £100 and the race became 'a sweepstake of ten sovereigns each' with £180 added. The owner of the second would receive no prize but his stake would be returned.

At the same time it became a weight-for-age race; four-year-olds carrying 11 st, five-year-olds 11 st 7 lb, six-year-olds and over, 12 st. A further innovation was the appointment of an umpire to ensure an orderly parade and a fair and punctual start.

Some authorities assert that the race was run at Maghull, on land owned by John Formby, whose wife's father had bought part of the manor of Maghull from the Molyneux (Sefton) family in the eighteenth century. That races were held there before Aintree cannot be doubted. But the Formby-organised races ended in 1835, conceding bitter victory to the Lynn-organised races at Aintree.

Lynn had the powerful patronage of Lord Molyneux, heir to the Sefton earldom. By 1835 he had forced Formby out of business and held control of all racing in Liverpool.

T. H. Bird in *A Hundred Grand Nationals* drew from local sources when he suggested that the race in 1837 was held at Aintree although it might have extended into Maghull. His sources were local newspapers of the time. They reported the race as being held at Aintree but did not mention Maghull. *Bell's Life* also mentioned Aintree.

But Aintree or Maghull, what does it matter? It was Lynn's race and Aintree was his place. He fought to establish it despite growing opposition.

This opposition had local roots, for it was at a Liverpool dinner-party in 1808 that guests decided to form a society for 'Preventing Wanton Cruelty to Brute Animals'. Their immediate concern was the protection of working horses on Merseyside and their exposure of cruelties affronted people in all walks of life.

The Liverpool society was short-lived, but the seed was planted. In 1822, when 'Humanity' Martin, the Member for Galway, tried to persuade Parliamentary support for his 'Ill Treatment of Horses' Bill, the controversy crackled like a forest fire. The Bill was lost between the House of Commons and the House of Lords, but Martin tried again, extending his Bill to include cattle, and even—to the amusement of Members—asses. In 1823 his Bill got through both Houses, partly because of the persuasive support of Edinburgh-born Lord Erskine, who had for years tried to protect horses from abuse.

The Bill made it an offence wantonly and cruelly 'to beat, abuse or ill-treat any horse, mare, gelding, mule, ass, cow, heifer, steer, sheep or other cattle'. The minimum penalty was a fine of 10s, the maximum a prison sentence of two months. Sentences varied according to the sympathies of magistrates, but coachmen, committed to fast times by their employers and carters compelled to over-loads and quick deliveries, were among the early victims of a law which seemed to discriminate against those who drove for a living.

There were growls of protest when a carter was judged guilty of whipping a tired horse up a long hill while 'gentlemen riders' continued to whip and spur tired horses over walls and fences. It seemed to the cynical that all was permissible provided it was indulged by the privileged and called a 'sport'.

In 1824 the Society for the Prevention of Cruelty to Animals was formed. Royal patronage was not given until 1840, but during the 1830s the society demonstrated its resolution in a series of prosecutions. By 1837 it had become a powerful influence, with supporters in the twenty-four towns where steeplechasing was established.

It was against this background that Lynn introduced his race of two circuits and four miles. Its date was the day following Coleman's big steeplechase at St. Albans, which might explain the small field and the absence of Captain Becher.

Riders were allowed to inspect the course on the morning of the race, but the umpire was given authority to order them to start at 'a reasonable time' and to declare those who did not start 'as distanced'. The first umpire was Viscount Molyneux.

This was another example of Lynn's flair. First the confinement of the race to an enclosed course; then the attempt to ensure orderliness and punctuality. They were signs that Lynn was aware of his public and determined to please.

The hot favourite was Dan O'Connell, a small chestnut owned by Mr. Knaresboro and the first Irish horse to contest the Grand National. Other horses were The Disowned, Zanga and Mr. Sirdefield's The Duke, described by the *Liverpool Standard* as a 'hunting cob' and ridden by Mr. Henry Potts.

There was a false start and a broken stirrup leather caused long delay. Finally the runners got away 'pretty fairly', with Dan O'Connell making the early running. The course crossed a turnpike road and 'the leap into the road was rather steep'. All got over it and crossed to the biggest fence of the race. Fronted by a wide ditch, it was a bank about six feet high with a fringe of thorn. This was the Trial fence. Dan O'Connell took one look and persistently refused. The rest of the field stopped also.

The Duke jumped at the second attempt, 200 hundred yards clear of The Disowned. Zanga followed some minutes later, but dislodged his rider at the next.

With one circuit completed, The Duke, going an easy gallop, led The Disowned 'by about fifty yards'. They returned to the Trial fence and jumped without hesitation. The Duke continued clear to the final flights of hurdles, and the local *Standard* reported: 'The pace now became very severe, The Disowned fetching up his advantage.' The reporter added a comment which fed the flames of controversy: 'The horses were nearly abreast, the riders punishing them severely.'

But Alan McDonough could get no more out of The Disowned. Two hundred yards out it was all over. The Duke won 'by about thirty yards at a severe pace'. An estimate of the time was fifteen minutes.

The Duke passed to Mr. Chawner, in whose name he was to run the following year, but there's good reason to suppose that in 1837 he was the property of Mr. W. Sirdefield, who owned the George Inn.

Mr. Sirdefield, therefore, became the first owner of a National winner, while Henry Potts became the first winning rider. Born in Denbighshire in 1810, Mr. Potts was twenty-seven, a bachelor, riding without the consent of his parents and only because another rider had withdrawn through illness. He retired from racing when he married. His winter home was Watergate House, Chester, and his hunting stables were at Beeston. He died in 1884.

The year: 1838
Number of runners: Ten
Winner: Sir William (A. McDonough—12 st)

The town authority withheld financial support perhaps because of rising criticism. The only added money was £25, given presumably by William Lynn. The race remained a sweepstake of ten sovereigns each, but the Trial fence was lowered while others were so reduced that they were described as 'low with blind ditches'.

Again Lynn was making concessions. His first need had been to persuade public support. This year his need was to guarantee a spectacle by attracting more horses. Owners were not prepared to risk their horses or riders their necks over a fence which had daunted even Dan O'Connell.

The lowering of the Trial fence was one reason for the increase in runners from four to ten. Another was the decline of the rival race at St. Albans. Coleman's sun was going down. In 1838 Lynn's sun was still high. Only he knew how much it was costing and within a year he would be admitting total disillusion.

The Duke was 2—1 favourite. He was ridden by Captain Becher, who had been at St. Albans the previous year. Mr. Potts attended the meeting but had no ride.

It's in the details of this second Grand National that the official record quarrels with the Liverpool newspapers of 1838. The official record gives Sir Henry as the winner, ridden by Oliver; an error which might have been introduced in 1867, when the newly formed National Hunt Committee first produced an authoritative record of steeplechases. Later it published *Winners of the Grand National since 1867* and in

1900 reached further back to earlier winners to make its published record comprehensive.

By then the race of 1838 was sixty-two years old. Presumably records were inadequate or memories shaky. Certainly the statement that the winner was Mr. Thompson's Sir Henry, ridden by Oliver, was not derived from local newspapers at the time. Liverpool newspapers agreed that the race was won by Mr. McDonough's chestnut gelding Sir William, ridden by the owner. Mr. O'Moor's Scamp, five years old and carrying 10–12, was second. The Duke, given variously as running in the name of Mr. Sirdefield and Mr. Chawner, was third.

This is the version which T. H. Bird preferred in *A Hundred Grand Nationals*. On page 21 he stated: 'There is no evidence that any horse called Sir Henry ran at the meeting or that Tom Oliver... was riding there.'

It might be that Bird's trust in newspapers of the early nineteenth century was exaggerated. They made mistakes; events were reported by the untrained or semi-trained; it's improbable that any Liverpool reporter of 1838 knew much about steeplechasing. But if their reporting is accepted Sir William became the first Irish horse to win and Alan McDonough became the first owner-rider. For The Duke it was a first of another kind. He broke down in the final stages to become the first casualty.

The year: 1839
Numbers of runners: Seventeen
Winner: Lottery (J. Mason—12 st)

Three days before the race William Lynn announced his retirement and added: 'A number of the most influential noblemen and gentlemen, patrons of the Turf, anxious that the Liverpool meetings should be conducted with the same respectability and spirit by which they have hitherto been distinguished, think it a fitting opportunity for placing the future arrangement of the races on a more secure and permanent footing than individual enterprise could effect.'

He announced the formation of a syndicate of '1,000 proprietorships of 25 sovs each'. The Trustees were Lord Stanley, Sir Thomas Massey Stanley, and Messrs. Aspinall, Earle and Blundell. The race committee comprised the Earls of Derby, Sefton, Eglinton and Wilton; Lords George Bentinck, Stanley and Robert Grosvenor; Sirs John Gerard, Thomas Massey Stanley and R. W. Bulkeley; the Hon. E. M. Lloyd Mostyn and Mr. E. G. Hornby.

The public explanation was that Lynn's health was failing, but in a private letter he described the Aintree venture as 'a most unlucky speculation for me. I should have been worth at least £30,000 if I had never had anything to do with it.' He shared the disillusion of Tom Coleman and John Formby, unaware that the race which he had introduced would survive 130 years and two world wars as well as storms of controversy and an appeal to the House of Lords.

Details of a sweepstake of £20 each, forfeit £5, with £100 added, were published on January 6th and attracted a total entry of fifty-three. During the week of the race public interest was without precedent. Liverpool hotels were fully booked. A local newspaper gleefully reported that guests would be sleeping 'four to a bed'. The eclipse of Coleman's race at St. Albans meant that London as well as the North and Midlands looked to Liverpool for the big steeplechase of the year.

On Tuesday, February 26th, the roads to Aintree were 'crowded with pedestrians . . . piemen, chimney sweeps, cigar sellers, thimble riggers and all the small fry of gaming-table keepers'. No vehicle could be hired. Half a guinca could not buy a place on crowded omnibuses. The stands were crowded at seven shillings a ticket. Spectators clung to roof-tops, chimneys, trees. Squires on horseback waited to follow the runners towards the ploughed fields. A contemporary estimated 'not fewer than forty to fifty thousand persons on the ground'. Their control was entrusted to special constables. Pickpockets and tricksters had a field day.

The Courier reported: 'The town has been perfectly alive with bustle. Visitors from all quarters and by all sorts of conveyances, from North and South, from Scotland, Wales and

Ireland by steamers, railways, coaches, chaises, gigs and waggons. Our inns have been crowded with gentle and simple; the taverns and private houses have been everywhere in request for the accommodation of the sporting fraternity of all descriptions. . . . The mansions of our country gentry have been crowded with guests, who have exhibited their "swell turn-outs" in our streets, jostling the equipages of our merchants.'

The Courier also reported brisk betting at the Talbot Hotel the previous evening, 'though it was greatly held in check by the uncertainty as to what horses would start. The entry exhibited a list of fifty-five horses. The Nun was installed favourite, with plenty of support for Rust, Daxon, Seventy-Four, Cannon Ball, Paulina and Railroad.' (Other sources give the total entry as fifty-three.)

The race should have started at one o'clock. Two hours later the runners were still parading. The Nun was found to be 'rather too fat', and Alan McDonough put her to 'some severe galloping before the race, probably with a view to getting her in wind'. Despite this drastic treatment she remained favourite at 6—1. Lottery was reported to be 9—1 and *The Courier* counted 'horses to the number of eighteen' going to the start. The official figure is seventeen.

'Captain Becher on Conrad led the way at a slapping pace. . . . Through the first three or four pasture-fields there was nothing but extremely light fencing, and the horses topped in gallant style everything that stood before them. The first obstacle that wore the aspect of a teaser was a deep ditch, above five feet wide, on the further side of which was a high bank. The high-mettled fellows made nothing of this—they flew over like birds and were presently labouring through a deep, light soil, from which young wheat was springing. They next dashed over a high bank into a grass field, where Captain Becher was still looking back at his competitors, Daxon, Lottery, True Blue, Dictator and Paulina in a line behind him.'

Part of the course was heavy plough and the pace slowed. Becher rode Conrad towards the next fence: 'First there was a strong paling, next a rough, high, jagged hedge, and lastly a brook about six feet wide. . . . Captain Becher, on Conrad, smashed through the palings and rolled over into the brook.' History was made, the fence was named. Becher would win immortality in failure as Henry Potts would not in victory.

Lottery led the others over the crouching Becher, 'letting him feel the wind of their heels'. But Becher was not finished. He caught Conrad and remounted, riding with such purpose that he was in the lead again as they approached 'a high hedge, bank and rails, on the other side of which was a piece of water, let in for the purpose, full fifteen feet wide, the field adjoining which is six feet lower than that from which the leap was to be taken'.

Becher was willing but Conrad was not. He had 'no mind for such exertion' and 'tumbled headlong into the water, rolling over his rider and floundering about after a most extraordinary fashion'. Rust was another victim, but his rider retained the reins and remounted.

The wall before the stands was formidable; five feet high, built of stone and topped by turf. 'Lottery in particular flew over like a cat. It was observed that the fencing of this horse throughout was most splendid.' The reporter could not know that another legend was being made.

Lottery continued to lead The Nun and Paulina on the second circuit 'till they came to the great leap at the piece of artificial water before-mentioned. Dictator, ridden by Carlin, took the leap about ten yards further on than the rest of the field. He got well over, but from some cause or other stumbled and fell headforemost on the opposite side. He was all in a heap and it was plain that he was much strained.'

But there was no reprieve for poor Dictator. Hauled to his feet, he was remounted and sent in pursuit. 'The next very awkward leap, however, finished him. He sprung over the rest but instantly fell and died almost immediately. It is stated that his back was broken.' In that sentence the reporter gave ammunition to those who declared all steeplechasing, the Aintree race in particular, to be an affront to humanitarian principles.

Lottery won 'with apparent ease, beating Seventy-Four by

several lengths'. Paulina was third and True Blue fourth.

Lottery was bred by Mr. Jackson at Riston Grange, near Hull, and originally ran under the name of Chance. He won a race at Holderness in 1834, but seems not to have raced again until 1836, when Mr. Jackson took him to Horncastle fair in Lincolnshire. Horse-dealer John Elmore was there, looking for horses capable of jumping.

Elmore sensed a bargain and instructed his groom to try the 'mealy brown colt' over a post and rails. Lottery jumped with an aptitude which suggested that properly schooled he would 'jump from hell to Hackney'. Elmore paid £120 and took him home to Uxendon, near Harrow-on-the-Hill. Lottery's education included two mile steeplechases and hurdle races at Bayswater Hippodrome, an enclosed track near London which John Whyte had introduced to satisfy public enthusiasm. Lottery also ran on the flat, but failed in the St. Albans race of 1838.

There was good reason for his failure. A nineteenth-century writer, 'Argus', described it as Elmore's biggest mistake, for Lottery was 'dead amiss and a fortnight before was almost a corpse'. But Elmore was more a judge of a horse than a horseman. He 'never spared horses and had to have a run for his money'.

In 1839 Elmore sent Lottery to Epsom to be trained by George Dockeray, a flat-race jockey who had won the Derby on Lapdog. It was from Epsom that Lottery came to Aintree for the third Grand National, then went on to win at Cheltenham, Stratford-on-Avon, Maidstone and Dunchurch. After the Dunchurch race Alan McDonough declared: 'Lottery must be the best horse in the world, for he could trot faster than any of the rest of us could gallop.'

The greatest tribute was paid by organisers of a meeting at Horncastle. The conditions of a race read: 'Open to all horses except Lottery.'

3

As soon as the 1839 race was over, the Trustees began to prepare for 1840. 'Upwards of fifty gentlemen' subscribed to ensure that the 1840 race would be 'one of the most splendid ever witnessed, whether as regards the patronage it will receive or the number of horses that will be entered'.

The stone wall, retained to please Irish owners, was lowered to four feet six inches and an 'ox-fence' added 'to give Leicestershire horses an equal chance'.

Its title was the 'Grand Liverpool Steeplechase', but an anonymous contributor to *Bell's Life in London*, reporting the 1839 race, had already called it the 'Grand National'.

The year: 1840
Number of runners: Thirteen
Winner: Jerry (B. Bretherton—12 st)

Lottery was an early favourite, despite a penalty of 7 lb which increased his burden to 12 st 7 lb. But there was plenty of support for The Nun, beaten the previous year, and for the Irish horse Valentine, who gave his name to Valentine's Brook.

The 'whisper' on the day was for Jerry, apparently owned by Lottery's owner John Elmore, although there was no registration at that time. Horses changed hands frequently and Jerry was bought and sold so often that doubt persists about his ownership in 1840. Bird wrote in *A Hundred Grand Nationals* that Jerry was almost certainly 'Lord Suffield's property when he won the Grand National, though he was allowed to run in the name of Mr. Villebois, presumably the Norfolk squire who lived at Marham and hunted his own staghounds, and who was also constantly engaged in transactions with Elmore'. On the other hand Irish journalist O'Leary in *Grand National* attributed Lottery's comparatively long odds to the 'rumour that John Elmore had declared to win with Jerry. A declaration, which is no longer allowed, gave the owner of two horses in one race permission to win with one above the other if they were fighting out the finish.' The official record also gives Elmore as the owner, with no hint that Lord Suffield or Mr. Villebois were in the background.

It was to prove a race of accidents, the first of many Nationals to be reduced in one minute from tense struggle to tragic fiasco. Lottery made the early running, pursued by Mr. Power on his own horse, Valentine. The Irishman had boasted in Dublin that at all costs he would be 'first at the wall'. For this reason the early pace across the wheatfields was fast enough to spread-eagle the others. Only Lottery could stay with Valentine.

They were side by side as they approached the wall. An eye-witness reported that they reached it together. In that moment the sequence of disasters began.

The previous year Lottery had jumped a higher wall with contemptuous ease. Now he faltered. Perhaps he'd been 'taken off his feet' by the early pace. Perhaps he was bumped or impeded. Whatever the reason, he scarcely rose. To the horror of the crowd he struck the wall and toppled over. He tried to struggle up as Columbine and The Nun jumped. Lottery rose into them. They struck him down, then fell near him.

Mr. Won, the rider of Columbine, was the first to recover. He reached a crouching position, too dazed to understand the warning cries. Seventy-Four jumped the wall and struck him an 'oblique blow'. He dropped as though shot. Seventy-Four fell on Columbine.

Only five were left standing. Valentine was among them,

ahead of Jerry and Arthur. At the first of two hurdles in the straight Valentine was still in front and Mr. Power was within inches of a greater victory than his original intent to be 'first at the wall'. But he paid the penalty for his break-neck pace. Valentine faltered and Jerry went by. Arthur, ridden by Alan McDonough, put in a strong challenge without reaching Jerry. The horse who had failed as a hunter drew away to win with comparative ease.

Arthur took the second prize of £30, while Mr. Power on Valentine saved his stake. Two others, Lord Waterford's The Sea and Mr. Whitaker's Cruickshank, completed the course. The Nun never recovered from the accident at the wall, but rider Powell, a 'tough customer' from Gloucestershire, was luckier. He came back to win in 1841.

It was the end of Lottery as 'the best horse in the world'. He was to run again at Aintree under crushing weights, but like Golden Miller nearly a hundred years later he seemed haunted by the memory of failure.

The year: 1841
Number of runners: Ten
Winner: Charity (Mr. A. Powell—12 st)

The wall was removed and a water-jump substituted, but the damage was done. Those who had never seen a steeplechase were dismayed by what had happened to Lottery and The Nun. They became part of a semi-articulate agitation against all steeplechasing, some of it from within Liverpool.

The *Liverpool Mercury* had already made its opinion clear: 'We can be no more reconciled to it . . . than we are to cock-fighting, bullbaiting, or any other popular pastime which is attended with the infliction of wanton torture to any living being. That these steeplechases are of this nature will hardly be denied even by those who are most ardently attached to such sport.'

It was not easy to attribute opposition to hysterical cranks. No less an authority than Nimrod, who wrote for *The Sporting Magazine* and had no qualms about blood sports, despised steeplechasing as 'cruel and perilous'. The injuries to Lottery and The Nun, following the death of Dictator in 1839, gave topical force to the protests and must have alarmed the organisers of the race. They might not all have shared William Lynn's flair for publicity, but they were aware that the race could not prosper without public approval.

Inevitably there were armchair riders, as brave and as eloquent as armchair soldiers, who denounced the removal of the wall and stressed that the Liverpool race would be diminished if it ceased to be the severest test of horse and man. But it could have been no coincidence that the field of 1841 was seven less than in 1839 and included no new horse of outstanding ability.

Lottery was given 13 st 4 lb, including a penalty of 18 lb for winning at Cheltenham. It was a tribute and at the same time a sentence. With such a burden Lottery was condemned to failure before the flag went down. Ridden by Jim Mason, he tried to stay with the leaders but the pace set by Lord Craven's Charity was too hot. Mercifully Mason acknowledged it. He pulled up to save Lottery unnecessary punishment, a gesture less common then than now.

Seventy-Four, another survivor of the 1840 disaster, was close up, accompanied by Cigar, Peter Simple, The Hawk, Revealer and Goblin. But when Charity reached the hurdles in the straight the mare had only Cigar and Peter Simple to beat.

For Charity this was a second time at Aintree. She'd run in 1839 when ridden by Mr. Hardy and had won on the flat as well as over hurdles. The first mare to win the National and owned by Lord Craven, who became the first peer, she was ridden by A. Powell.

Cigar was second and the Peter Simple who finished third was not the horse who won in 1849 and 1853. The Peter Simple of 1841 was a grey by Arbetus and a winner in the Midlands.

The year: 1842
Number of runners: Fifteen
Winner: Gay Lad (T. Oliver—12 st)

Some sources name horse-dealer John Elmore as the owner of Gay Lad, but again there is doubt about who owned the horse at the time of the race or in whose name he ran. Some reports attribute the nomination to Mr. D'Arcy.

Elmore had two other runners: Lottery, whose popularity with the National-day crowd was little diminished, and Sam Weller, ridden by Barker. All were well backed at the Talbot Hotel during the evening before the race. Public loyalty to an old favourite was such that Lottery was backed down to 5—1, with Gay Lad 7—1 and Sam Weller 8—1. Peter Simple, third the previous year, and veteran Seventy-Four were other popular choices.

Sam Weller was an early faller and Peter Simple, going such a gallop that Mr. Hunter could not settle him, jumped in breakneck fashion until baulked by the crowd. Lottery ran well but was spent when Mason pulled him up. Experts thought he was again beaten less by the pace than by the weight.

Powell, who had won on Charity the previous year, took up the running on Seventy-Four. A mile out, Seventy-Four seemed a certain winner, jumping with such ease that Becher's became just another fence. But he tired during the run-in and stumbled at the last hurdle, where Tom Oliver pounced.

Oliver had first attracted attention when riding Seventy-Four behind Lottery in 1839. Now he proved himself a worthy rival to Mason by driving Gay Lad to win by four lengths. Seventy-Four hung on to finish second, two lengths in front of Peter Simple.

Tom Oliver was nicknamed 'Black Tom'. It was said at the time that he was 'born in debt' and 'lived in debt', without apparently giving a damn. Extravagant and generous, he squandered the considerable sums which he must have won in a long career. Born at Angmering, in Sussex, he drifted to Ireland in search of fortune, then returned to Liverpool with three-halfpence in his pocket. After a term as rough-rider, he became a 'gentleman rider' in name and a hard-bitten professional in fact. The crowd loved him for his cheerful impecunity as much as for his gypsy appearance. Debt finally landed him in Oxford prison, where he wrote to a friend that his greatest need was a 'good wall jumper'.

The year: 1843
Number of runners: Sixteen
Winner: Vanguard (T. Oliver—11st 10 lb)

It was 'Black Tom's second successive triumph, lifting him to a rare place among Grand National riders. It was also the year in which the race became a handicap and its title 'The Liverpool and National'.

The Sporting Magazine described the entry as 'a string of horses never congregated together in the palmiest days of steeplechasing. Lottery, Peter Simple, The Returned and Consul were of themselves sufficient to draw a host of admirers.'

For the first time there is mention of a race-card, giving the names of the horses and the names and colours of the riders. The card also provided a map of the course, showing 'the fences, artificial hurdles, walls, lanes and brooks to be encountered'. Some changes had been made. The artificial brook 'opposite the winning chair' was widened 'from twelve to thirteen feet more than last year' and the wall was restored, four feet high and padded with turfs.

The race was scheduled to start at three and was only twelve minutes late. This might have been due to the efforts of William Lynn, who remained a prominent organiser although he had relinquished sole control. *The Sporting Magazine* reported him 'indefatigable in his exertions to keep order, clear the course and the enclosures in front of the Grandstand—no very easy task'.

When Lord Sefton got the runners away, Peter Simple, third in successive years, was 3—1 favourite. Lottery was second favourite at 4—1, despite his failures and because his weight had been so reduced that he was receiving 9 lb from the favourite. Vanguard was 20—1.

Peter Simple again set a scorching pace, fighting for his head and giving jockey Frisby a rough ride. The wall claimed several casualties and Lottery, perhaps remembering the disaster of 1840, narrowly avoided jumping on the fallen. Dragsman ran out, clearing a gate and dashing along a lane before his rider could recover control. Despite this, the Cheltenham horse fought his way back into the race and was there with a chance as the leaders approached the final hurdles.

Vanguard jumped the last better than Nimrod and Tom Oliver was too strong and clever to allow this advantage to be lost. He drove Vanguard home by three lengths from Nimrod, who held off the challenge of Dragsman by only half a length.

Lord Chesterfield, the owner of Vanguard, was the second peer to win the National. He was also among the first flat-race owners to take more than passing interest in steeplechasing. Despite its popular appeal, the sport was still a disreputable off-shoot of flat-racing. Most steeplechase meetings were poorly conducted, without central control and virtually ignored by the Jockey Club.

Aintree, however, had become a proud place. The stands were complete; the course was prepared in a form which would not be drastically changed in more than a hundred years. Bird, in his volume to commemorate the centenary, emphasised the contribution made by Lynn, who 'had laid his foundations very well; the edifice was complete, and the rest of the work was for the decorators in embellishing and strengthening the structure'.

The year: 1844
Number of runners: Sixteen
Winner: Discount (*Mr. Crickmere—10 st 12 lb*)

Horse-dealers were attracted to steeplechasing for two reasons. They were shrewd in recognising a potential jumper and slovenly supervision invited the chicanery for which horse-trading was notorious.

After the chain of successes attributable to John Elmore came Mr. Quartermaine, a horse-dealer of Piccadilly. He owned a horse called Discount who had raced unsuccessfully as Magnum Bonum and had changed hands for £80. Discount was a newcomer to Aintree, but despite his success he never came back.

Lord Craven's Charity was again trying to repeat the success of 1841. She was low in the handicap with 10 st 7 lb. Others who knew their ways around were Peter Simple, The Returned and The Romp; while on the morning of the race there was a strong 'whisper' for Lather, owned by Lord Edward Russell and so terrified of trains that he could not be loaded to travel by rail. He had been walked to Aintree and seemed none the worse.

For the first time the race was run in heavy rain. The crowd was small. Those who braved favourite vantage-points near the canal and Becher's could see little. A grey curtain obscured much of the course. Those in the stands saw little more, despite their telescopes.

Tom Tug, ridden by Rackley and owned by horse-dealer Tilbury, was the popular choice. In ordinary conditions he would probably have won. He took his usual hold during the first circuit, almost dragging Rackley's arms from their sockets, but deep mud sapped his strength. With a mile remaining he was exhausted, while reports suggest that Rackley was little better. The jockey was 'in a fainting condition' and had to be 'lifted off the horse' at the finish.

Discount won from The Returned with Tom Tug third. Caesar was fourth and Lather, despite his long walk, fifth. Peter Simple, The Romp, Nimrod and the gallant mare, Charity, were among the fallers.

This was the year in which Lottery ran his last race. He won at Windsor on April 8th, 1844, and subsequently became a hack. Epsom trainer Dockeray rode him on the Downs for some years, but there was no honourable retirement for 'the greatest horse in the world'. Lottery spent his last days in the shafts of a cart at Neasden.

The year: 1845
Number of runners: Fifteen
Winner: Cure All (W. J. Loft—11 st 5 lb)

Again the weather seriously affected the race. For days there had been deep frost, so roughening the ground that the race was run only after consultation with owners. The start was delayed until five o'clock.

Peter Simple ran well. Less impetuous with age, he was beaten two lengths by Cure All, a £50 horse when bought from a Northamptonshire farmer the previous year. Again there is doubt about ownership. In his year of triumph Cure All ran in the name of Mr. Crawford, but was wholly or partly the property of his rider, in whose name he was to run the following year. Mr. Loft was well known in Lincolnshire, and the county celebrated his success.

The year: 1846
Number of runners: Twenty-two
Winner: Pioneer (Taylor—11 st 12 lb)

This was the 'five miles National', when a mistake in flagging extended the course and produced a winner who'd been thought to have 'no more chance than a donkey'.

Cure All, the winner in 1845, shared top weight with Lord Howth's Switcher and Lord Waterford's Firefly, but none paid much attention to Pioneer, a six-year-old bay gelding by Advance, sire of the 1843 winner, Vanguard. In the pre-race betting Pioneer was not even quoted, while during the parade he was thought to be a 'rough-looking fellow, in poor condition'. Even his owner, Mr. Adams, despised his chances. Yet Pioneer proved a run-away winner, shocking the crowd to silence as he sprinted away on the flat to win by three lengths from Culverthorpe and Switcher.

It was a 'course fit only for heroes' and The Scavanger didn't take long to realise it. He refused at the first. Hornihiharriho, nicknamed 'Hurry Harry' by the bookmakers, fell and kicked jockey Parker in the face. Lancelot collided with a spectator who ran across the course. Tom Oliver was thrown by Carlow, while Veluti, ridden by Jim Mason, broke down. Loft pulled up Cure All when the gelding was exhausted by the extra mile. Others were kept going until they fell. They included Peter Simple, Mameluke, Regalia, Tinderbox, Brenda, Pickwick and Troubadour.

Captain W. Peel subsequently paid £1,000 for the winner, but Pioneer never showed such devastating form again. He ran in 1847 and was fourth. In 1848 he broke down.

The year: 1847
Number of runners: Twenty-eight
Winner: Matthew (D. Wynne—10 st 6 lb)

Since 1839, when an unknown reporter had first used the phrase, the people of Liverpool had called their race 'The Grand National'. In 1847 the title became official.

The largest field so far included Brunette, a thirteen-year-old mare ridden by Aintree veteran Alan McDonough. There was a prejudice against black horses. They were supposed to be excitable and timid. But this black mare by Sir Hercules had proved a prolific winner in Ireland when owned by Mr. Knaresboro, whose Dan O'Connell had proved the first Irish failure at Aintree.

She dominated the parade. By comparison another Irish horse, Matthew, looked poor; mealy brown in colour and mean of manner. But big steeplechases are not won by looks. Lottery had been dismissed as mealy brown and poor, while the winner of 1846 had looked gypsy rough and in 'poor condition'. Shrewd judges realised that Matthew was by Vestris and had that bold, confident eye which was to become a characteristic of Aintree-type horses.

Many of the shrewd judges were Irish and they got their money on in a hurry. The crowds 'followed the money' to make Matthew odds on at 10—11.

Others in the field were Jerry, who had won in 1840; Pioneer, the 1846 winner; and Culverthorpe, who had finished second to Pioneer. The way they out-jumped and out-stayed a formidable field provided further evidence that some horses showed their best at Aintree.

Matthew, owned by Mr. Courtney and ridden by the Irish jockey, D. Wynne, won from St. Leger and Jerry. Pioneer was fourth and Culverthorpe fifth.

It was a disastrous race for bookmakers but the mail-boats were singing all the way to Ireland. There was a joke at the time that if Matthew had not won half Ireland would have emigrated.

The year: 1848
Number of runners: Twenty-nine
Winner: Chandler (Captain J. L. Little—11 st 12lb)

Twenty-seven-year-old Captain Little was a former officer of the King's Dragoon Guards who had lost his money in a bank failure and been relegated to the 81st Regiment of Foot. He bought a half-share in Chandler from Captain Peel, who also owned Pioneer.

Chandler had been once owned by a chandler of Sutton Coldfield. He'd changed hands for sixty guineas and been hunted for three seasons before going to Hednesford for training. When running second at Warwick he was said to have jumped thirty-seven feet. But neither horse nor rider was considered experienced enough for Aintree.

Matthew, the 1847 winner, was among the runners. So was Pioneer. Formidable Tom Oliver was riding The Curate, while John Elmore had a new horse, The British Yeoman, who attracted support because any Elmore horse must be worth a bet.

For the third time in four years the weather was the enemy. Heavy rain churned ploughed fields to mud. In such going 'anything could happen'. An early accident put Matthew out of the race. He was brought down when 'going like a lion'. Pioneer collapsed. Meanwhile Chandler kept pounding, well handled by Captain Little, who had been coached by Tom Oliver.

Ironically teacher and pupil were in close rivalry at the last. The Curate jumped boldly and Oliver seemed to have the race won, but his pupil came from behind with a well-judged run to win by half a length. The British Yeoman maintained Elmore's record by finishing third.

The year: 1849
Number of runners: Twenty-three
Winner: Peter Simple (*T. Cunningham—11 st*)

The decade ended as it had begun; with a series of disasters, never forgotten by those who saw the race and never forgiven by those who opposed it. Three horses were killed. The immediate assumption was that they had fallen victims to the huge obstacles and the first protests were aimed at reducing their severity. In fact the obstacles were low banks of dark earth, apparently insignificant, even scorned by those who walked the course in the morning.

Horses fell heavily because the banks were not severe enough to challenge a good jumper, or because they were of dark earth, the same colour as the fields and indistinguishable. It was claimed that horses did not see them until the last second.

The race began badly and—like other races of the future—did not recover. Lord Sefton's signal was misunderstood and some of the horses were left. Those who got away went too fast, as though afraid of re-call. The sequence of accidents began to mount. Kilfane was killed. The Curate, second in 1848 and ridden by Powell, broke his back. So did Equinox. To the horrified crowd it seemed the course was as littered as a battlefield.

Peter Simple made much of the running to win easily from The Knight of Gwynne and Prince George. The winner, frequently confused with the grey who had run prominently but unluckily several years earlier, was owned in 1849 by Mr. J. F. Mason. In 1853, when he won for the second time, he ran in the name of Captain Little.

Subsequently Cunningham told a story of attempted bribery during the race. When it was obvious that Peter Simple would win, another rider shouted to Cunningham, offering £1,000 to pull the horse. As Peter Simple drew away, the shout became fainter and the offer larger; going up to £2,000, £3,000, £4,000. To his credit, if not to his profit, Cunningham shammed deafness and rode his horse into history.

4

The Crimean War (1854–6), in which Britain was allied with Turkey, France and Sardinia against the Russians, directly affected steeplechasing. Young officers found their excitement and action at Balaclava, leaving steeplechasing to professionals who masqueraded as amateurs.

This was one cause of the decline during the 1850s. Another was the eruption of small meetings, as many as fifteen in a month. There were not enough horses or accomplished riders to ensure good fields in so many scattered places. Moreover, organisation was so casual and deception so common that steeplechasing was becoming discredited among all save the credulous.

Ironically a sport which had survived persistent and powerful opposition was being destroyed by its own shortcomings. Only the Grand National retained its stature, although the smoke of scandal was to blow around it intermittently. During the 1850s the average number of runners was twenty-two, four more than the average for the previous decade.

The year: 1850
Number of runners: Thirty-two
Winner: Abd El Kader (*C. Green—9 st 12 lb*)

Mr. Joseph Osborne, an early contributor to *Bell's Life* and compiler of *The Horsebreeders' Handbook*, became the first writer to own a National winner. His Abd El Kader was little more than 15.2 hands high, the smallest horse to win until The Lamb in 1869. There's a story that the dam of Abd El Kader was discovered by Mr. Osborne's father in the team drawing a coach from London to Shrewsbury. Mr. Osborne senior bought the mare for forty guineas and bred from her. Abd El Kader was her eighth foal, as vicious as he was small, considered a 'weed' until he was put to hunting. He proved so clever over any type of obstacle that Joseph Osborne began to hope he might win a race. His steeplechasing career, beginning at Worcester, graduated to Aintree where none of the experts would look at him.

The popular choice in a field of thirty-two—a number unequalled until 1909 and not surpassed until 1921—was Peter Simple, an easy winner the previous year and again ridden by Cunningham. Chandler was also there, ridden by Captain Little. Bottom weight was The Pony at 8 st 7 lb, while there was plenty of support for The Knight of Gwynne, second in 1849, and for Lord Waterford's Sir John.

To the astonishment of the crowd and the delight of the Irish, who could claim that Mr. Osborne's father had lived at Dardistown Castle, Co. Meath, Abd El Kader galloped a class field to a standstill. Carrying only 9 st 12 lb, compared with the crushing burdens which had been inflicted on Lottery, he finished so full of running that he 'might have galloped the course again'.

The Knight of Gwynne held on to finish second with Sir John third. They were followed by Tipperary Boy, Farnham, Maria Day and Vengeance. Among the fallen were Chandler, Rat Trap, Spring Buck and Rainbow.

The year: 1851
Number of runners: Twenty-one
Winner: Abd El Kader (*T. Abbott—10 st 4 lb*)

Abd El Kader became the first to win the National twice and the first to win in successive years. The handicapper treated him kindly, adding only 6 lb for his victory in 1850, yet he started at the surprisingly long odds of 7—1.

There were those who thought he might win again without 'blowing enough to put a candle out', but the one-time 'weed' who had been rejuvenated by hunting had a tough race this time. There were only inches in it at the finish and in the closest finish so far the winning margin was officially returned as 'half a neck'.

The mare Maria Day, ridden by the veteran Frisby, who had ridden the grey Peter Simple, was second and might have won but for a mistake at the last. Sir John was again third. The favourite, Rat Trap, ridden by Mason, got round. So did Vain Hope, ridden by Sam Darling.

Abd El Kader ran again in the Nationals of 1852 and 1853, but when travelling by train to Liverpool in 1854 he broke free, so damaging himself that he was thought unlikely to race again. Yet race he did, returning to Aintree in 1858 in the ownership of Mr. Briscoe. He fell at the second fence.

That was the end of his Liverpool career, but he continued to win minor races and became the last horse Jim Mason ever rode. Mason came out of retirement to ride a match against The Clown, but by then Abd El Kader was only a shadow of the horse who had won the National twice in succession. There were rumours he had been 'got at'.

The year: 1852
Number of runners: Twenty-four
Winner: Miss Mowbray (A. Goodman—10 st 4 lb)

The water jump, placed as now in front of the stands, was declared to be dangerous. The allegation provoked a letter from Lord Sefton to *Bell's Life*:

'It is stated that the water jump opposite the Grandstand has been altered by my instructions, and that it was thus made a large and dangerous leap. This is not at all correct. In the constant preparation of this artificial fence the workmen had gradually diminished the depth of the ditch till it had become a

Easter Hero (F. Rees up) the 'best horse never to win a National'. He was retired to America by owner Mr. J. H. Whitney

Kilmore leads over the last to win the National of 1962. He gave Fred Winter a second winning ride

Poethlyn wins for the second time. His 1918 win was at Gatwick. In 1919 he won the first post-war National at Aintree. Ridden by E. Piggott, he achieved the rare distinction of winning in successive years

Red Alligator (B. Fletcher), extreme left, was almost brought down at Becher's in the 1968 race. He got through the muddle to win easily

A near disaster for the Scottish favourite Freddie during the 1966 race. Jockey Pat McCarron pulls him out of danger as four crash at Becher's. Freddie finished second to Anglo

Chaos at the twenty-third in 1967. Horses break through the fence after the riderless Popham Down crossed the leaders. Foinavon kept clear of the shambles to win

mere splash of water, and I desired that it might be restored to its former dimensions in every respect. This was done and no more.'

He described the water as '13 feet six inches in breadth and no more than 4 feet deep. The rail is about 3 ft high, strongly made and leaning towards the water. It is a very large but perfectly fair leap.'

Abd El Kader, attempting his hat-trick, was handicapped at 11 st 4 lb, giving 20 lb to the favourite, La Gazza Ladra, and 32 lb to the bottom weights. For much of the race he seemed likely to do it, but the early pace was too fast, the weight proved too much and Wynne pulled him up.

At Valentine's, Chieftain led from La Gazza Ladra, Sir Peter Laurie, Maurice Daley and an unknown mare called Miss Mowbray, ridden by Alec Goodman, a thirty-year-old farmer from Peterborough. Approaching the final hurdles Miss Mowbray out-galloped, then out-jumped them all to win by a length from Maurice Daley. Sir Peter Laurie was third. Chieftain, La Gazza Ladra, and Sir John were others to finish, followed by Warner, ridden by W. Archer whose year was to come.

Miss Mowbray became the second mare to win, confounding the judges, who thought her a 'rat of a thing'. She was bred in Bedfordshire by Mr. Boulton, but no one wanted her as a five-year-old; not even the Manchester businessman who bought her for 100 guineas, then rejected her as unsound. Mr. Boulton could not find another buyer until Mr. J. F. Mason, who had already won the National with Peter Simple, rode her to hounds with the Oakley. He offered a fair price and with some relief Mr. Boulton sold.

Miss Mowbray won the Warwickshire Hunt Cup for her new owner, but when she came to Aintree she was so little considered that her name did not appear in the return of starting prices.

The year: 1853
Number of runners: Twenty-one
Winner: Peter Simple (T. Oliver—10 st 10 lb)

It was Peter Simple's second success in five years and another for 'Black Tom'. The old mud-larker had passed from Mr. Mason to Captain Little, but Mr. Mason became the first to own second and third.

One of his horses was Miss Mowbray, but Alec Goodman preferred Oscar, her light-weight stable companion. Long frost, followed by thaw, made the going heavy. They were the conditions Peter Simple had been waiting for since 1849.

Abd El Kader, his weight down to 10 st 10 lb, made the early running but again he failed to stay, finishing a tired fifth. Peter Simple splashed home by three lengths from Miss Mowbray, with Oscar three lengths away third. The top weight, Sir Peter Laurie, was fourth.

It says much for the consistency of these Aintree 'specialists' that the first, second and fifth places went to the winners of four previous Grand Nationals. Such consistency gave effective answer to those who insisted that the fences were dangerous and that horses were destroyed by them.

The year: 1854
Number of runners: Twenty
Winner: Bourton (Tasker—11 st 12 lb)

There were ugly rumours of corruption during the weeks before the race. Miss Mowbray, now trained at Epsom by Dockeray, who had prepared Lottery for the National of 1839, was a popular choice. 'List houses' encouraged ante-post betting and the tide of money for Miss Mowbray was without precedent, although her price fluctuated ominously. Bookmakers who made her a cautious favourite one day were joyfully extending the odds the next. Rumours that those closely connected with the horse were backing her as 'a certainty' were contradicted by rumours that she was lame or sick and would not run. She seemed well when sent from Epsom to Liverpool. Apparently she arrived without injury. Yet half an hour before the start she was found lame.

The crowds were incensed. The suspicion that Miss Mowbray was the first National favourite to fall victim to foul play deepened to certainty when the trainer declared that at some time and unknown to him, the mare had been blistered. This is the application of a counter-irritant, and is an acknowledged treatment for damaged tendons. Needless application would inflict pain and minor lameness.

Dockeray had no alternative save to withdraw the mare, but the questions of the crowd remained unanswered. Who had done it? And when? Few needed to ask why, for ante-post bets were forfeited. The public suspected that it had been robbed to bookmakers' profit.

This incident and its undertones did much to encourage the belief that steeplechasing needed to impose self-discipline if it was to escape suicide. But the appointment of a governing committee, capable of introducing and implementing sensible rules, was delayed more than ten years.

Oscar, third the previous year, was among the early casualties when brought down by Peter Simple. The winner was Bourton, owned by Mr. W. Moseley and ridden by Tasker, who was killed at Warwick the following year. Bourton had a margin of fifteen lengths over Spring, owned by Mr. J. Barber and ridden by W. Archer. Crabbs, ridden by Denis Wynne, was third, ahead of the headstrong Burnt Sienna, Lady Arthur and Half-and-Half.

Bourton had been once called Upton. He had run at Liverpool in 1852 and 1853, when ridden by Sam Darling, but after his victory in a fast time he was sold by Mr. Moseley to a man in Leamington. Presumably his legs were near break-down, for the sum was only £50 and the agreement, spoken or implied, was that the new owner should give the horse 'a good home'.

The agreement was broken, the new owner declaring that the horse had 'done nothing to entitle him to become my pensioner for life'. There was less sympathy for him than there should have been, since Mr. Moseley had had the best and whoever takes the best must incur a debt. Any 'pension for life' should surely have been given by the owner who had won the greatest steeplechasing prize of the year.

In the hope of getting either sport or profit for his outlay, the Leamington gentleman brought Bourton back to racing at Warwick and engaged Sam Darling to ride. The horse broke a fetlock at the water jump, lashing about in such pain and rage that Darling could not get near him. By a coincidence his National jockey, Tasker, was also killed at Warwick.

The year: 1855
Number of runners: Twenty
Winner: Wanderer (J. Hanlon—9 st 8 lb)

The weather was bad, the going heavy. They would have been ideal conditions for mud-lark Peter Simple, but the bay winner of two Grand Nationals in seven attempts was at last retired. In his absence there were only three capable of giving their best in mud. They were Maurice Daley, strongly fancied the previous year; six-year-old Free Trader, sired by The Sea who had finished the course in 1840; and the Irish horse Wanderer, lightly handicapped and backed by his owner, Mr. Dennis, at 25—1.

The favourite, Trout, owned by Mr. Moseley and ridden by Tasker, was among the early fallers. So was Bastion, giving Tom Oliver his seventeenth successive ride in a National. Little Charlie, a newcomer who was to have his day in 1858, was brought down, while Miss Mowbray, the second mare to win and the first favourite to be nobbled within hours of the race, fell heavily at Becher's and had to be destroyed.

Wanderer, believed to be a descendant of Eclipse, won by two lengths from Free Trader, with Maurice Daley third. Both winner and second were stallions, although it was the custom then as now to geld horses for steeplechasing.

The year: 1856
Number of runners: Twenty-one
Winner: Free Trader (G. Stevens—9 st 8 lb)

Free Trader was handicapped at only 9 st 6 lb despite his close second to Wanderer the previous year. No less surprisingly, he was 25—1.

It was a first success for George Stevens, who liked to ride a patient race, letting others go on and make mistakes while he kept out of trouble during the first circuit. Mr. W. Barnett, who owned Free Trader, gave Stevens a present of £500. Cheltenham, his home-town, presented him with a watch. It was a romantic triumph for the boy who had run away to become a jockey. Stevens' confidence in his destiny was justified, for he was to win four more Grand Nationals and become the greatest horseman of the nineteenth century.

Minerva was second and Minos third. Two future winners, Emigrant and Little Charlie, were still standing at the finish; and the French participated for the first time. Baron Lamotte sent over Franc Picard and Jean du Quesne. The latter was well backed and ran promisingly until fading near home.

The year: 1857
Number of runners: Twenty-eight
Winner: Emigrant (C. Boyce—9 st 10 lb)

For several years there had been growing criticism of the weight-range. Supporters of the R.S.P.C.A. might have supposed that to lower the maximum weight and to have the minimum as low as 8 st 10 lb was to be merciful to horses over four miles and so many fences. It was not as simple as that.

One effect was to exclude some of the best riders, few of whom could scale less than eleven stone. Those who had gained experience at Aintree before the weights were altered were confined to the top weights or squeezed out. Lightly weighted horses were ridden by inexperienced jockeys or by grooms; none of whom had the skill to 'think' such a race or to keep a horse out of trouble. There was reason to suppose that some of the disasters were caused less by the severity of the fences than by inexperienced light-weights taking too many risks.

The Sporting Review complained: 'The Liverpool steeplechase weights are sillier than ever, running from 11—2 to 8—10. In fact, Oliver and the leading steeplechase jockeys have hardly a chance of a mount, and the struggle is left to some wretched ex-racers ridden by ex-jockeys and some light grooms. Alas that Liverpool—which has seen Lottery carry his 12 stone over its walls—should have sunk so low.'

The lament was specious, since it ignored the fate of Lottery in 1840, but it expressed a growing grievance. For two years the National had been won by horses carrying less than 10 st. There were many owners of weight-carrying stayers who echoed the comment: 'Well may gentlemen refuse to send anything like a weight-carrying hunter to be beaten in the run in for speed.' The magazine thought that those receiving as much as 30 lb from the top weights were 'betting office trash who could not live two miles under 11—7'.

Emigrant, handicapped at 9 st 10 lb, was no 'betting office trash' as Ben Land, jockey and trainer, could have pointed out. In his autobiography George Hodgman told how, when staying at the George Hotel, Shrewsbury, he heard Land exclaim, 'If things go on like this I shall have to sell Emigrant!' Land was playing cards at the time and 'things' must have gone from bad to worse, for he sold the horse to Hodgman for £590 and lived to lament his luck still further.

Emigrant had run unsuccessfully in 1856 and his weight in 1857 was reduced from 10 st 2 lb to 9 st 10 lb. Hodgman backed the horse to win a fortune, although he must have been frightened a week before the race when jockey Boyce injured an arm in a hunting accident.

The arm did not respond to treatment, but Boyce concealed the injury, riding with the arm strapped to his side to perform one of the oustanding feats in the history of the race.

His skill and strength justified Hodgman's tribute that Boyce was 'so far the best . . . that I should not care to select a second'.

The owner's gratitude was further expressed in a gift of £1,000; which confirmed other jockeys in the belief that to win the National was their only short-cut to big money. Rewards for winning most steeplechases were derisory compared with the gifts to flat-race jockeys.

Emigrant won by three lengths from Weathercock. By one of the best ironies which the race has produced, Weathercock was owned by Ben Land who had sold Emigrant when the cards turned cruel.

Previous winner Free Trader and future winner Little Charlie were among the fallers. So was Minos, third the previous year and made favourite on that form. Albatross dropped dead. The French horse, Jean du Quesne, now owned by the Count de Cunchy, again got round to finish sixth.

The year: 1858
Number of runners: Sixteen
Winner: Little Charlie (W. Archer—10 st 7 lb)

Snow lay thick on the Aintree course, blown into drifts as deep as graves. The race was delayed three days in the hope of improvement, but the snow was still whirling and the wind still screaming as sixteen assembled for the start. Spectators were estimated at only 500. They were so scattered around the circuit that Aintree seemed as empty as a graveyard. Some Frenchmen were among them, for Weathercock, second the previous year, had been bought by the Vicomte Talon in earnest indication of the French intent to win.

It was a day for accidents. Bird described it as 'disastrous . . . the worst Grand National up to that date'. Little Tom fell on the first circuit and was remounted to fall headlong into the water. Tom Oliver was concussed when Escape came down. Lough Bawn, ridden by George Stevens, refused. Treachery was pulled up.

But tough Little Charlie would not give in. He'd served an apprenticeship in previous Nationals and knew his way around. Tribute was paid at the time to the careful riding of William

Archer, who'd been riding since early boyhood and was as tough as his horse.

Little Charlie won easily from Weathercock, with Xanthus third. The history of the race is littered with good horses who jumped consistently and ran bravely without finding the luck to win. Weathercock was one. Xanthus was another.

Archer eventually retired to the King's Arms, Prestbury, near Cheltenham, where he taught his sons, William and Fred, to ride over hurdles. The elder son, William, was killed by a fall at Cheltenham, while Fred became champion flat-race jockey at seventeen, winning 2,748 races, including twenty-one classics, before his death in 1886.

The year: 1859
Number of runners: Sixteen
Winner: Half Caste (*C. Green—9 st 7 lb*)

Only twenty-two years had passed since the first Grand National, but newspapers were already complaining that the race was not 'what it used to be'. Some blamed the weight-range; others the gradual adjustment of the most criticised hazards; a few the loss of genuine amateurs to military service abroad.

Public support declined, partly because Aintreee seemed chronically unlucky in its weather, partly because steeplechasing in general was in the hands of the unscrupulous. The scandal of Miss Mowbray, heavily backed, then surreptitiously lamed when the jockeys were about to weigh out, was not readily forgotten.

The Sporting Review commented: 'No fair bet can be made on a steeplechase owing to the number of accidents which take place but it offers ample employment for the sharper and such as have no vast amount of character to stand upon.' The magazine added the hope that steeplechasing would not 'become a lasting amusement of the people of England. Already it has begun to decline in popularity.'

Only sixteen horses faced the starter, twelve less than in 1857. Xanthus, Little Charlie and Weathercock were among them. So was Claudius, ridden by Tom Oliver. Half Caste, a six-year-old who had fallen in his only race over fences, was the mount of C. Green, the rider of Abd El Kader in 1850. The French threat was continued by Jean du Quesne, ridden by Lamplugh. Few took much notice of a mare called Anatis, ridden by 'Mr. Thomas'. The rider's real name was Thomas Pickernell, of whom the Duke of Hamilton wrote to Dick Marsh: 'Mr. Pickernell was the finest man over a Grand National course I ever saw.'

The quality of the field was declared to be mediocre, yet the finish was the closest so far. The Brewer fell at the water. Xanthus, Little Charlie and Weathercock went at various stages, while Tom Oliver ended his Aintree career when Claudius came down. The French began to cheer as Jean du Quesne reached the last hurdle full of running, but it was then that Half Caste, handicapped at 9 st 7 lb, fought a long duel to win by a short head.

Anatis was fifth. The mare pulled up sore, her legs so tender that she did not appear on a racecourse until the National of 1860. It was said that in the meantime she was not even risked over a schooling fence and that her preparation was confined to a few half-speed gallops.

The decade ended in a sour mood. The time for reform was near. The angry and disgusted were about to unite in a sustained attempt to impose the discipline without which the sport could not survive.

5

In 1860 *Baily's Magazine* campaigned for the establishment of a controlling body, associated with and recognised by the Jockey Club but independent of it. In the words of *The History of Steeplechasing*, more than a hundred years later: 'Many owners of hunters and steeplechasers had utterly disregarded any decisions made by local stewards, whose authority was limited. Any suspension of jockeys for foul riding, or of owners or trainers for flagrant abuse of the conditions of races, could only be effective at the meetings under their control. There was no liaison between the various clerks of courses.'

Bell's Life, joining *Baily's Magazine* in the fight, printed a code of laws and regulations, some of which were approved by Admiral H. Rous, senior steward of the Jockey Club. But the attitude of the Jockey Club to steeplechasing continued to be condescending at best and negligent at worst. Even when a committee was formed to govern steeplechasing as for many years the Jockey Club had controlled the flat, there was no great unity of effort. For about twenty years the National Hunt Committee remained a lesser body, faced with the gruelling task of making their regulations work.

A preliminary committee was formed in 1863, largely at the instigation of Mr. B. G. J. Angell, who was to win the National with Alcibiade in 1865. He had the support of Mr. W. G. Craven, a member of the Jockey Club. Lord Grey de Wilton was co-opted and for two years they struggled against prejudice and special interests to get their published rules accepted. In 1866 the National Hunt Committee, with the reluctant approval of the Jockey Club, was formally appointed. In alphabetical order its members were: B. J. Angell, C. H. Carew, Viscount Chaplin, Lord Coventry, Captain H. Coventry, W. G. Craven, Sir Frederick Johnstone, Captain J. Little, G. Payne, Lord Poulett, A. Summer, Lord Westmorland, Lord Grey de Wilton. They were joined by the Duke of Beaufort in April 1866, and by Viscount Suffolk and E. C. Burton in 1867.

It was a powerful committee. Captain Little and Captain Coventry had ridden in Grand Nationals. Lord Poulett was to win the National with The Lamb in 1868 and 1871. As a rider in Ireland, he had once ridden six winners in an afternoon. George Payne was a former master of the Pytchley Hunt.

One of their earliest tasks was the definition of 'gentleman rider'. The term had come to mean very little. Professionals had ridden in the National from the start, although a condition of the race had been its confinement to 'gentlemen'. Tom Oliver, for instance, had returned penniless from Ireland to become a 'gentleman rider' and simultaneously one of the best professionals of that time.

The National Hunt Committee confined 'gentlemen' to members of stated Hunt and London clubs or to 'officers on full pay in the Army or Navy, or persons holding commission under the Crown, or bearing titles in their own right, or by courtesy'. Others 'not qualified as above' were asked to send 'their names to Messrs. Weatherby's office, proposed and seconded by persons qualified as above, and a ballot will take place from time to time'.

This attempt to define and to segregate was received with indignation. One correspondent asked 'why a member of the Reform is a gentleman and a member of the Conservative is not?' The committee was accused of being more meddlesome than constructive, but proof of its growing effectiveness against rogues and swindlers was its request for co-operation from the Steeplechase Society in France so that horses and owners disqualified in either country could not cross the Channel.

Slowly the sport ceased to be 'synonymous with robbers . . . got up for the most part as an instrument of fraud and barefaced swindling'. At the same time the Grand National was restored to its former stature. The most important decade in the history of steeplechasing was to see a series of noteworthy Grand Nationals and the emergence of two of the greatest long-distance steeplechasers of all time.

The year: 1860
Number of runners: Nineteen
Winner: Anatis (Mr. Thomas—9 st 10 lb)

High gales blew Aintree sideways, again reducing the crowd to the hardy few who would brave any hardship for the biggest spectacle of the year. The field included Xanthus and Goldsmith. George Stevens rode Maria Agnes, while Tom Pickernell, still masquerading as 'Mr. Thomas', was there again with Anatis. The mare's legs were known to be so rickety that few could have rated her highly against Jealousy, judged by Stevens to be a probable winner although he could not claim the ride.

Xanthus set a fast pace, with Jealousy and Goldsmith among the fallers. Anatis was not prominent until they turned away on the second circuit. Then she began to make steady headway, finally to win by half a length from Huntsman, ridden by Captain Townley.

There's a story that in the straight Townley called across to the rider of Anatis: 'Is a thousand any good to you, Tommy?' It was the second time a flagrant bribe was reputedly offered during the running. As on the previous occasion, it provoked only a greater determination to win.

Xanthus was a tired third, followed by Maria Agnes, Irish Boy and Brunette. The last-named was bought by Mr. Rowlands, an amateur so determined to ride a National winner that he had backed himself to win £5,000. Bridegroom struggled home with another amateur, 'Mr. Ekard', a plausible inversion which concealed the identity of Mr. Drake of Shardaloes. In these casual times it was as correct to ride under an assumed name as it remains to write or to act.

The year: 1861
Number of runners: Twenty-four
Winner: Jealousy (J. Kendall—9 st 12 lb)

The opinion of George Stevens was vindicated. The previous year he had thought Jealousy a probable winner and was not deterred by the horse's failure. Given a choice of thirteen for the 1861 race, he chose Jealousy with the repeated assertion that given ordinary luck Mr. Bennett's horse must win.

Unhappily there developed one of those involved wrangles to which racing is prone. Stevens had obligations to other owners who refused him permission to ride for Mr. Bennett. The result was that he became a spectator. J. Kendall, who had got Brunette round the previous year, was engaged.

There was a record entry of eighty-nine and the field of twenty-four was the highest since 1857. Among them was Old Ben Roe, scratched from all engagements under the name of Joe Maley but allowed to run under a new. Such an irregularity would soon be illegal.

There was a fall before the start. Lord Sefton was thrown by his hack as he led the parade, but 'was able to get back to the paddock without assistance'.

Xanthus set his usual pace, but by now the public recognised him to be one of those who would never win. Valentine came down at Valentine's, getting a leg entangled in the reins. The Conductor fell and was remounted by Nightingall. He fell again to be fatally injured. Cockatoo came down and blundered into gallant Anatis, back again despite her legs in an attempt to win in successive years. She kicked fallen jockey Green, who had been out of luck since winning on Half Caste.

Brunette, bought by Mr. Rowlands to win a private bet, fell at a ditch. Xanthus faded as they approached the run-in and was passed by Jealousy. Kendall kept Jealousy in front to win by two lengths from The Dane and Old Ben Roe. Bridegroom was fourth.

Again the winner was handicapped at less than ten stone and again critics scorned a weight-range which penalised the genuine stayer who was up to weight.

The year: 1862
Number of runners: Thirteen
Winner: Huntsman (*H. Lamplugh—11 st*)

The superstitious were to know this as the year of 'unlucky thirteen'. James Wynne was killed in front of the stands. He was the son of Denis Wynne, who had ridden odds-on Matthew in 1847. On the morning of the race he received news of the death of his sister. Lord de Freyne, the owner of O'Connell, offered to release Wynne, but the Irishman would not forgo the chance of emulating his father.

For years critics of steeplechasing had predicted tragedy, believing that formidable fences must at some time demand a formidable toll. Yet the disaster was at an innocuous fence and caused by the fall of another horse. Playman, ridden by Nightingall, hit the gorse and came down, bringing down Willoughby. O'Connell crashed into Willoughby and Wynne's injuries to ribs and chest were such that he died during the night.

Among the fancied was Thomastown, owned by Tom Naghten and sent from Ireland to be ridden by Murphy. There was support also for Huntsman, second in 1860 and recently bought by Vicomte de Namurs, who was determined to win the race for France.

Anatis was again among the early leaders, but Tom Pickernell pulled her up when she was plainly leg-weary. Xanthus tried again and jumped the course, but by now he had few pretensions to speed. The race was won appropriately by the 'best horse in it', ridden by Lamplugh who had been second on Jean du Quesne in 1859. Huntsman became the first French-owned horse to win and Lamplugh became the first French jockey.

Three years were to pass before the first French-bred horse succeeded.

The sport had become popular in France as well as in Germany, but at home the storm was at its height. Twenty years ago it had been criticism from without. Now it was criticism from within. Much of it was aimed at the Aintree fences and Aintree handicapping.

Organisers were accused of pandering to the new type of steeplechaser; a reject from the flat who had been hunted seldom if ever, bred for speed and able only to jump 'garden fences . . . fit for a boy on a pony'. Angry voices within the sport insisted that the original purpose was being lost. Genuine steeplechasers were being discouraged. *Baily's Magazine* declared: 'We must have the weights up if steeplechasing is to go on as the sport of gentlemen.'

Despite the muddle of accusation and derision, during which *The Sporting Review* described many of the Aintree fences as 'most contemptible', the only immediate concessions to weight-carrying stayers were the lifting of the minimum weight to ten stone and the extension of the distance from four miles to four miles and a half.

The year: 1863
Number of runners: Sixteen
Winner: Emblem (G. Stevens—10 st 10 lb)
Time: 11 minutes 20 seconds

There was an air of celebration about this year's event, for the Prince of Wales and Princess Alexandra had been married the previous day. Queen Victoria had allowed it to be a national holiday, although she remained in mourning at Windsor. The North extended the holiday to 'National day', and the crowds were such that it became known as the 'Picnic National'.

The field of sixteen included a remarkable mare called Emblem, bred by Mr. Swale, of Saredon, near Wolverhampton, and sired by Teddington who had won the Derby for Sir Joseph Hawley. At three years old Emblem was bought by Mr. Halford and ran thirteen times on the flat with only one success. Lord Coventry bought her for 300 guineas and sent her to Golby at Northleach, Gloucestershire, to be schooled over fences and hunted in the Cotswolds. Emblem was a slow and reluctant learner, described as 'a weedy sort' who 'couldn't win the price of a saddle'.

Her owner, only twenty-five at the time, was among those who were campaigning for reform and would become a member of the National Hunt Committee. His reputation was such that almost all the money was for Emblem at 4—1. It was less a tribute to the horse than a vote of confidence in Lord Coventry.

Ridden by George Stevens and handicapped at 10 st 10 lb, Emblem received 18 lb from the top weight. Medora was ridden by Fothergill Rowlands, a doctor in Monmouthshire who had abandoned medicine for steeplechasing. Jealousy was another fancied runner, but the race was marred by accidents.

The Orphan, having been led to the start, reared and sulked, then refused to take part until his chance was lost. Inkerman crashed and galloped riderless, interfering with the leaders until running out. His determination to get away from Aintree was such that O'Leary wrote of him: 'He was not found until nightfall some miles away from the course.'

The Dane, second in 1861, broke his back. Jealousy, Avalanche, Fosco and Yaller Gal followed Arbury towards the final hurdles, while Stevens persuaded Emblem into a position to strike. It was another National to be won as much by rider as by horse. For more than four miles Stevens had ridden quietly, saving yards and giving his mare plenty of time to see each fence. Now he drove her forward to take the lead at the last hurdle.

Emblem responded willingly, then startled the crowd by flinching sideways. A lesser rider might have been unseated or rattled, but Stevens got her over, then kept her going to win by twenty lengths from Arbury and Yaller Gal. It was Stevens' second win.

The year: 1864
Number of runners: Twenty-five
Winner: Emblematic (G. Stevens—10 st 6 lb)
Time: 11 minutes 50 seconds

Emblematic was a sister to Emblem and was also owned by Lord Coventry, who became the first peer to win in successive years. He had bought Emblematic from Mr. Halford for 250 guineas and she had immediately proved clever over fences 'with splendid shoulders and a very deep chest with long and powerful quarters'.

Again there was popular support for a horse in such ownership and again the victory of a flat-race thoroughbred carrying only 10 st 6 lb infuriated those who considered that the richest prize in steeplechasing should be won by steeplechasers. Not since Bourton in 1854 had a horse won with more than eleven stone.

A critic wrote bitterly that far from being a fair test of a steeplechaser, the Aintree course was 'full of ploughed fields and in the back stretch by the canal there seemed to be nothing else'. It was a condemnation in key with an opinion expressed in *The Sporting Review*: 'It almost requires a microscope to discover the fences.'

Yet it was a race of many accidents, two falling at the second fence and bringing down others or so impeding them that afterwards they were not seen with a chance. Jerusalem, the favourite, fell twice, and at the finish only five were standing.

Arbury, second the previous year and ridden by Ben Land, was the only serious challenger to Emblematic. The mare, hard trained by E. Weever at Bourton-on-the-Hill and so spindly of leg that paddock judges had doubted she would stay the distance, came away to win by three lengths. Chester, an unconsidered outsider, lumbered into third place, followed by Thomastown and Ocean Witch.

Stevens, the second jockey to win in successive years and the second to win three times, had backed Emblematic to win £300. Lord Coventry had also backed her to win £500 on behalf of the jockey. Stevens used the money to build a cottage on the top of Cleve Hill, Cheltenham. He called it 'Emblem Cottage'.

The year: 1865
Number of runners: Twenty-three
Winner: Alcibiade (Captain Coventry—11 st 4 lb)
Time: 11 minutes 16 seconds

The work of Mr. Angell's committee was showing results. *Baily's Magazine* declared: 'Three years ago Aintree was said to be on its last legs. . . . Noblemen and Gentlemen, it was said, would no more subscribe to the Grand National than they would take shares in a hazard bank.' Now the efforts of a few were being rewarded and 'by careful and constant watching it may be said to have become as healthy and flourishing as before'.

Appropriately the winner was owned by Mr. Angell, who had formed the original committee in 1863.

Alcibiade was the first French-bred horse to win and the first five-year-old. He had never before run in any steeplechase, while his rider, Captain Coventry of the Grenadier Guards, had ridden in few races. The combination of young horse and inexperienced rider frightened off support and pre-race betting was for Emblem, Emblematic and L'Africain. Dark rumours surrounded the French horse L'Africain. He was injured on the journey to Aintree and declared unfit. Those with long memories remembered Miss Mowbray. Again the sport was damaged by rumours which might have been without foundation.

In the final stages the race was between Alcibiade, representing the new type of Aintree horse, and hunter Hall Court, representing the old. The race from the last hurdle was described in *Gentlemen Riders Past and Present*: 'The roar that went up from the stands, and all along the line as Alcibiade and Hall Court, jumping the last hurdle almost together, leaving Emblematic, the favourite, toiling hopelessly in the rear, raced up the straight side by side; the grim look of determination on the face of Mr. Coventry as hard at work with whip and spur he called on Mr. Cherry Angell's horse for all he was worth, the despairing glance of Captain Tempest as the game son of Cossack and Aunt Phyllis, responding to call after call from his rider, drew up inch by inch to win eventually by the shortest of heads, was an incident which will never die out from our memory.'

Stevens kept Emblematic going to finish third, but Emblem was among the fallen. Mistake was fourth, Merrima fifth and Flyfisher sixth.

Captain Coventry became the first 'swell of the Guards' to ride the winner, but he did not ride in the National again. After the race it became known that Alcibiade had not been as untried as might have appeared. He had been schooled at Lubenham and tried in private against Bridegroom, second to Huntsman in 1862. Bridegroom was a genuine horse, ideal for a trial, and Alcibiade had always got away from him. The secret was well kept and Mr. Angell's horse started at 100—7.

The year: 1866
Number of runners: Thirty
Winner: Salamander (A. Goodman—10 st 4 lb)
Time: 9 minutes 58½ seconds

It was the most important year in the history of steeplechasing, for it saw the formal appointment of the National Hunt Committee as the acknowledged central authority. The rise in the status of steeplechasing was celebrated with a field of thirty, the highest since 1850.

The French sent over Laura, who became favourite. L'Africain, shown in the ownership of Mr. Powell, was set to carry 13 st 2 lb and Effenberg, owned by Count Furstenberg, 12 st 8 lb, although no horse had ever won with more than 12 st. Alcibiade and Hall Court, who had fought a memorable duel in 1865, were back; while Cortolvin, his year soon to come, and The Doctor, second to The Colonel several years later, were impressive newcomers.

There was also Salamander, handicapped at 10 st 7 lb and

ridden by Alec Goodman who had won on Miss Mowbray in 1852. Salamander was the horse with the crooked leg, bought in the words of *Baily's Magazine* 'out of a hovel in Ireland in much the same condition as a Lambeth casual'. What the hovel-bred 'cripple' did to a first-class field astonished a crowd of more than 30,000.

L'Africain fell, brought down in a ditch by another horse. Hall Court fell at the fence after Valentine's and Alcibiade did not survive Becher's. Bird wrote in *A Hundred Grand Nationals* 'It did not matter much, for nothing could have lived with Salamander.'

Goodman allowed him to take the lead as they approached the first of the hurdles and Salamander strode away to win by ten lengths from Cortolvin. O'Lynn, describing the finish in *Grand National*, wrote that Salamander 'with his heart of fire, was eased to a common canter to take the race and land a fortune for his owner'.

His owner was Mr. Studd, a retired indigo planter who had settled in Rutland, where he trained his own horses. The extent of his win so annoyed *Baily's Magazine* that it aimed the scathing comment: 'This gentleman's conduct in making the round of the bookmakers, and himself taking all the forties and fifties he could get, is, to say the least, rather paradoxical, and not the sort of thing we are accustomed to expect from the landed gentry of England.'

Mr. Studd's offence, apart from winning a great deal of money, was that he had run the horse at small meetings before the National, ensuring him steeplechasing experience without attracting attention. In this way he had deceived the handicapper, who might have heard the history of Salamander and despised him as a cripple.

Salamander was bred in Co. Limerick by Mr. Bouchier, whose family had been breeding horses on the Limerick grasslands for generations. He was a horse of the highest quality, but developed a deformity of one leg. Mr. Bouchier decided to sell at Mr. John Hartigan's 'Horse Repository' in Limerick. The horse didn't come up for sale. Mr. Hartigan spotted his potential and bought him privately for £35. Bird wrote: 'There have been a number of Grand National winners at one time and another bought for small sums, generally as yearlings, but no horse in the class of Salamander can ever have been bought for so low a figure.'

Mr. Hartigan turned the horse to grass for a while, unaware that Mr. Studd, who preferred to choose his horses rather than to rely on another's judgment, was on his way to Ireland. Studd and Hartigan met at Mullingar fair and the outcome of their meeting was that Mr. Studd bought three horses. Two were hunters. The other was meant to be a hunter, but turned out to be one of the best horses ever to win a National.

In a manner typical of betting owners, who persist in asking more and more, Mr. Studd did not let the National be the end of the season for Salamander. The following week the horse won at Warwick, again in a canter. Even that was not enough. In April Mr. Studd sent him to Somerset where he ran in a small race at Crewkerne. Salamander seemed to be winning as he liked until he fell at a small fence and injured himself so grievously that he had to be destroyed.

Another good horse who deserved better was L'Africain. He returned to France and broke a leg and a correspondent in Paris wrote of him: 'So his wretched career is over. . . . They pulled him, watered him when he was not thirsty, tempted him with beans when he was not hungry, pulled at him and raced him in wrong places. Then captains controlled him and touts tormented him. . . .'

Small wonder that for a moment the world of steeplechasing was ashamed.

The year: 1867
Number of runners: Twenty-three
Winner: Cortolvin (J. Page—11 st 13 lb)
Time: 10 minutes 42 seconds

Second the previous year when owned by Lord Poulett, Cortolvin had been sold to the Duke of Hamilton. A horse of doubtful pedigree, he had gained a reputation for being unwilling in a close finish. But the Duke thought Cortolvin could win, engaged his 1866 jockey, John Page, and backed him to win £11,000.

The experts were not impressed, preferring King Arthur, Shakspere, Astrolabe, and the five-year-old Fan.

Casualties were few, although old Thomastown, trying again with jockey Murphy, refused at the second. This was the fence to which Fan was to take repeated exception in future years. This time she jumped it easily and showed such promise that Mr. James, a professional owner, in the game for what he could get and making no bones about it, must have supposed her certain to win in the future.

On this day, however, nothing could catch Cortolvin. The supposed non-stayer won with 11 st 13 lb, the highest winning weight since the introduction of handicapping in 1843. Moreover, the time of 10 minutes 42 seconds was the fastest since the extension of the distance to four and a half miles.

Fan was second and Globule third. Six others got round and the agitation for stiffer fences was revived.

The year: 1868
Number of runners: Twenty-one
Winner: The Lamb (Mr. Edwards—10 st 7 lb)
Time: 10 minutes 30 seconds

It was a great year, not only because it was a great race but because it saw the emergence of a great horse. Experts preferred The Lamb to Salamander because of his short back and strong legs; the public preferred him to Miss Mowbray because he was small, only 15.2 hands high, as gentle as he was brave. His story began in Co. Limerick where so many of the best horse stories come from.

Mr. Courtney, the owner of Matthew in 1847, had a horse called Zouave, named in honour of the volunteers who fought for Pope Pius IX against Garibaldi. Mr. Henchy was his neighbour and Mr. Henchy had a mare, reputedly sired by Arthur, one of the earliest National horses and second to Jerry in 1840.

The horses were mated and the result was a small grey foal who became a pet of the Henchy family, especially of the delicate son. They called the foal The Lamb.

The boy died and The Lamb was sold at three years old for £30; £5 less than had been paid for Salamander in the same neighbourhood. The Lamb won a few races on the flat in Ireland and was offered for sale as an ideal ride for a boy. The price of £25 was considered too high. Mr. Studd, on one of his horse-buying visits, even dismissed him as too small and weak to 'carry a man's boots'.

Mr. Joe Doyle, a Dublin veterinary surgeon, knew better. He had already bought Thomastown from Tom Naghten in an unsuccessful attempt to win the National. Now he bought The Lamb and sent him to Punchestown to win the valuable Kildare Hunt plate.

This success persuaded Lord Poulett, who had sold Cortolvin a year too soon, that the little horse might be worth having. He leased The Lamb for the rest of his racing career and sent him to Ben Land, the jockey turned trainer who had sold Emigrant before the National of 1857. At the age of six The Lamb was prepared for Aintree and 'Mr. Edwards' was engaged to ride. It was the pseudonym of Hampshire cricketer George Ede, who owed his skill as a rider to the coaching of Land.

Chimney Sweep was favourite, with considerable support for Moose and Pearl Diver. The Lamb was at 10—1 with Fan and Helen. A high wind blew down tents and newspapers reported a pitched battle between the police and 'the roughs'.

Fan refused at the second fence and gave her name to it. For a reason never discovered she persistently refused to look at it, although the hope persisted that if she could be persuaded over it she would go on to win.

Alcibiade, the winner in 1865 and ridden by another Guards officer, Colonel Knox, was in the lead for a long time with Pearl Diver. Captain Crosstree, Astrolabe and Helen were also prominent, but when Pearl Diver drew away approaching the last only The Lamb had the strength and speed to go with him. The little grey hung on during the long run-in and George Ede got him in front when it mattered most to win by two lengths in the fastest time since 1863. Alcibiade was third, ten lengths away

The proudest man at Aintree must have been Ben Land. Nearly a hundred years would pass before another winning trainer could claim that he had also coached the winning rider.

The year: 1869
Number of runners: Twenty-two
Winner: The Colonel (G. Stevens—10 st 7 lb)

It's been often said that the best jockeys make the worst tipsters, but George Stevens again proved his flair as a judge of a horse. In a field which included Hall Court, Pearl Diver, Despatch, Fortunatus and Fan, he elected to ride a mongrel who had Exmoor ponies in his sire's pedigree and a half-bred dam.

The horse was The Colonel, bred and owned by Mr. Weyman and schooled by farm-workers on a farm at Brampton. The Colonel had inherited from his sire the pack-horse strength of the genuine Exmoor, and good judges in the paddock noted his tremendous back and short quarters.

Six days earlier he had won a hurdle race at Nottingham, where he had run in the name of Mr. Matthew Evans. This partly explains Stevens' interest, for he had married Mr. Evans' niece and knew all about the horse long before The Colonel came to Liverpool.

Globule made the running on the first circuit. Fan again refused at the second, to the despair of jockey Thorpe. Huntsman's Daughter broke a leg and jockey Wheeler was badly injured when Havelock fell. Gardener, Despatch, Q.C. and Alcibiade were there with a chance until Stevens made his move on The Colonel. For the fourth time he heard the cheers of the crowd as he stole the race from more flamboyant and excited jockeys.

Hall Court, again ridden by Captain Tempest, chased him home, followed by Captain Machell's Gardener.

Record books do less than justice to Hall Court, one of those sturdy triers who keep coming back to Aintree, never running a bad race yet never good enough. He had finished second to Alcibiade in 1865 and had fallen twice and finished seventh in following years. Now he was second to The Colonel, but still his Aintree career was not ended. The old horse was to come back in 1870 and public regard was to be expressed in his starting price of 40—1; long odds but considerably shorter than his 50—1 in 1865 and his 66—1 in 1869.

6

The 1870s began with the death of William Lynn, 'father of the Grand National' as Tom Coleman of St. Albans was the 'father of steeplechasing'. Like many of the horses which tasted fame at Aintree, Mr. Lynn ran out of luck in his later years. Not long before his death in 1870 friends subscribed a sum sufficient 'to enable him to live at home at ease and enjoy himself'.

The year: 1870
Number of runners: Twenty-three
Winner: The Colonel (G. Stevens—11 st 12 lb)
Time: 10 minutes 9½ seconds

The Colonel became the first since Abd El Kader (1850–1) to win in successive years. In the process he cut his time from 10 minutes 59 seconds in 1869 to 10 minutes 9½ seconds and gave George Stevens his fifth winning ride. The nomination was in the name of Mr. Evans, who seemed to have alternated ownership with Mr. Weyman. It was an arrangement less remarkable then than now and one of the laxities which members of the National Hunt Committee were resolved to eliminate.

Familiar names were in the race. Alcibiade, still trying to recover former glory, was 33—1 and gallant Hall Court 40—1. Fan, 11—2 the previous year, was out to 66—1. Pearl Diver seemed weighted out of it at 12 st 7 lb and the greatest threats to The Colonel promised to be The Doctor and Primrose.

Fan refused again. Hall Court was pulled up. Pearl Diver dropped jockey Page. Owner-rider Mr. Brockton kept Primrose in a strong lead from Alcibiade, Q.C. and Gardener. Casse Tête and Moose stayed with them for a while, then dropped out. Meanwhile Stevens on The Colonel was playing his usual game, following the maxim: 'Never be in a hurry to win.' But this time he found a rider waiting for him.

George Holman had nursed The Doctor through the first circuit as carefully as Stevens had nursed The Colonel. When the chips were down, The Doctor was still full of steam and as gallant as they come. Primrose went with them, but stumbled at the last flight. On the flat there was never more than inches between Holman and Stevens.

Stevens' riding was inspired. His strength and timing made the difference between narrow victory and honourable defeat. He got The Colonel home by a neck, with the young mare, Primrose, only a length away third.

It was one of the finest finishes ever seen at Aintree. Others to get round were Survey, Keystone, Gardener, Q.C. and the consistent Alcibiade, who had been third and fourth in previous years as well as successful in 1865.

The year: 1871
Number of runners: Twenty-five
Winner: The Lamb (Mr. Thomas—11 st 5 lb)
Time: 9 minutes 36 seconds

The Lamb had been excluded from the race in 1869 because of a wrong entry and Lord Poulett had elected to miss the race of 1870. But the gentle horse had retained his popularity with the Aintree crowd and was backed down to 5—1 despite the presence of The Colonel.

This was the confrontation which the crowds had been waiting for; the pony-sized winner of 1868 and the mongrel winner of 1869–70. Supporters of The Colonel pointed out that in 1870 he had carried 19 lb more than had The Lamb in 1868 yet had returned a time over twenty seconds faster. In addition he would be partnered by George Stevens, seeking his sixth win and helping to make the greatest partnership since Lottery and Mason.

The Lamb was ridden by Tom Pickernell (as 'Mr. Thomas') following the death of George Ede. In December Lord Poulett had written to Pickernell, confessing that he had dreamt of The Lamb's success: 'He won by four lengths and you rode him. I saw the cerise and blue sleeves, and you, as plain as I write this.... Say nothing to anyone.'

Presumably Pickernell said nothing, but you couldn't stop the crowds from backing their 'David' among the 'Goliaths'.

The start was delayed until 3.45 to enable Manchester businessmen to attend. They went to work in the morning, then hurried to Aintree, resolved not to miss what promised to be the race of the century.

It was a period of intense industrial activity in Lancashire. Prosperity touched areas which for generations had been dark with poverty. Suddenly there was money to spend and more than 100,000 crowded Liverpool on National day, 30,000 more than the total population of the town at the beginning of the century.

The stimulus to Liverpool trade was incalculable. The town was not yet a city, but it was growing rapidly as the 'cotton-port' of the North West. The feeling of prosperity was never sharper than during 'National week', when streets were crowded and hotels full and all means of transport were aimed towards Aintree.

In harmony with this feeling of prosperity the weather was so mild that Dick Marsh, riding Pulbrook, noticed picnic parties near the rail of the first fence and had to yell at them to scatter. Among the hazards of riding at Aintree were spectators who encroached on the course, leaning for a better view, then scampering across to friends on the other side. Not for many years would the whole of the course be railed off.

Pulbrook and The Doctor made the early running, but The Lamb faltered in the plough and for a time seemed to be out of it. He made up ground steadily towards the end of the first circuit while Stevens 'waited' on The Colonel in his usual way. The Doctor was pulled up at Becher's and fallen horses impeded The Lamb at the Canal. The little grey jumped over them with a hunter's dexterity and went on towards Valentine's with Rufus, Pearl Diver and Despatch.

The sunshine crowds looked back to The Colonel, waiting for him to come, still sure that the dual winner could come as soon as Stevens asked. But as The Lamb cleared Valentine's on the heels of Pearl Diver and Despatch, it became obvious that the long-awaited battle would not materialise. The Colonel was beaten.

From that point the crowds began to cheer, sure that nothing could catch The Lamb. Despatch tried to stay with him, but The Lamb had two lengths in hand at the finish. The time of 9 minutes 36 seconds was a record for a National of four and a half miles, no less than thirty-three seconds faster than The Colonel the previous year.

It was a devastating victory and crowds surrounded The Lamb as he reached the paddock. Souvenir hunters plucked hairs from his tail. Anonymous hands patted his neck and flanks. The Lamb bore the adulation patiently, while Lord Poulett came in for his share of congratulations. Not all the hands were innocent, for at some time during the mêlée he had his pocket picked.

The Colonel got round. So did Pearl Diver, Tusculanum, Rufus and Souvenance. The outsider Scarrington squeezed them out of third place.

That was the last Grand National in which George Stevens rode. He went back to Emblem Cottage and the expectancy of long retirement. But fate was waiting for him on Cleve Hill. He was riding his hack one windy morning when his hat blew off. A passer-by retrieved it, doubtless honoured to do so for Stevens was the idol of Cheltenham. He held it up, Stevens reached for it, and in that instant the horse bolted, galloping down Cleve Hill and turning so sharply that he slipped, throwing the hero of five Grand Nationals. Stevens' skull was fractured and he never recovered consciousness.

The year: 1872
Number of runners: Twenty-five
Winner: Casse Tête (J. Page—10 st)
Time: 10 minutes 14½ seconds

The Lamb was there again, his weight increased to 12 st 7 lb and his odds lengthened to 100—8, for even his greatest admirers could not imagine him winning a third National with such a burden. But his rival of the previous year was not there. The Colonel had been sent to Germany, where he became a successful sire at the Government stud at Beberbeck.

The race could have been won by Harvester or Scarrington. It went in fact to another flat-race reject, Casse Tête; only 15.3 hands high, one inch higher than The Lamb and in the same ownership as Pearl Diver.

Owner Mr. Brayley, who had twice seen Pearl Diver finish second, began with a Punch and Judy show, then graduated into show business before becoming a racehorse owner. He bought Casse Tête cheaply after the 'washy chestnut' had failed on the flat. There can be no doubt that his Pearl Diver was the better horse yet lacked the luck which left Casse Tête in front when Scarrington cut a leg at the last fence.

Harvester might have won but for the unluckiest of injuries. One minute he was full of running and Arthur Yates had visions of victory; the next he was hobbling, in such pain that Yates looked down to see blood on his trousers. He dismounted at once and lifted a foot. Harvester had twisted a plate; not a rare occurrence in steeplechasing and not enough to stop a gallant horse, as Easter Hero was to prove more than fifty years later. But this time a protruding nail had gashed another leg so severely that Harvester was splashing blood at every stride.

Primrose broke his back, while Lord Eglington's Schiedam, ridden by Maunsell Richardson, was brought down. Richardson was an all-round athlete, who 'won bets by jumping on to mantelpieces'. For a while he was to fill the gap left by the death of Charles Ede.

Casse Tête gave jockey Page his second winning ride. Scarrington, ridden by I'Anson, limped into second place, followed by Despatch. The Lamb was fourth and Fleuriste, ridden by the first Rickaby of three jockey generations, was among the finishers.

It was the end of the Aintree road for The Lamb. He was sold to Baron Oppenheim for £1,200 and followed The Colonel to Germany, where the sport was flourishing. Like many other horses before and since, he was asked to win one race too many and broke a leg and had to be destroyed.

The year: 1873
Number of runners: Twenty-eight
Winner: Disturbance (Mr. J. Richardson—11 st 11 lb)
Time: Not recorded

It was the beginning of what might be called the 'Machell era'. Captain Machell retired from the Army to live at Newmarket, where Machell Place near the town clock was named in his honour. He was a sportsman in the grand manner; larger than life, anything for a bet, capable of big generosity as well as towering fury. Once he won £1,000 in a walking match from Newmarket to London, using the money to buy three horses out of selling races. When the horses won, he sold them at a profit.

Another of his purchases was Disturbance, a former hunter who improved in Mansell's stable to become a possibility for Aintree. His greatest rival promised to be Rhysworth, but Mansell knew all about Rhysworth. So did Richardson, who was to ride two National winners for Machell. They knew that Rhysworth preferred to gallop alone, hating another horse alongside. Richardson's instructions were simple; keep with the second favourite in the hope of rattling him into error or of making him 'chicken out' when the pace began to hurt.

The tactic succeeded. Rhysworth gave in to persistent challenge and Disturbance, at 20—1, drew away to win by six lengths. The time was not recorded because the official watch failed. Columbine was third, while Star and Garter, Master Mowbray and Alice Lee were among the finishers.

Footman was a disappointing favourite. Prepared for the race by Weever, he fell on the second circuit at 'Fan's Fence', injuring his back and breaking two ribs. But these injuries were not discovered until a post mortem. In the meantime Footman had taken part in other races.

Captain Machell was not watching only his winner. He had an eye for Reugny, a five-year-old owned by Lord Aylesford and ridden by Joe Cannon. Machell bought him and turned him to grass, in readiness for another careful assault on the richest prize in steeplechasing.

The year: 1874
Number of runners: Twenty-two
Winner: Reugny (Mr. J. Richardson—10 st 12 lb)
Time: 10 minutes 4 seconds

Captain Machell became the fourth officially to own the National winner in successive years. John Elmore had triumphed with Lottery and Jerry in 1839 and 1840; Mr. Osborne with Abd El Kader in 1850 and 1851; Lord Coventry with Emblem and Emblematic in 1863 and 1864. Now the 'Captain of Newmarket' succeeded with the six-year-old who had run promisingly the previous year.

Machell also entered last year's winner, Disturbance, ridden by Joe Cannon, and Defence, ridden by Mr. 'Rolly', another assumed name. Casse Tête tried again, while the rider of Chimney Sweep was J. Jones.

Chimney Sweep seemed a certain winner after Valentine's on the second circuit, but Richardson made his move on Reugny in a fashion reminiscent of George Stevens. Reugny drew away to beat Chimney Sweep by six lengths with Merlin third, Defence fourth and Disturbance sixth.

To have three in the first six was a great triumph for the Limber Magna stable, yet the following day a notice appeared

Caughoo, the Irish outsider, crashes through the last to win in 1947. The margin was 20 lengths, the jockey E. Dempsey

Golden Miller, 'champion-of-champions', wins with ears pricked in 1934 in record time and despite a weight of 12 st 2 lb. Jockey G. Wilson looks over a shoulder for the closest challenger—Delaneige

Mr. What (Arthur Freeman) one of the 'grand old men' of Aintree, jumps Becher's in fine style to win in 1958

End of the road for tired Athenian, wedged in the nineteenth fence during the 1958 race. Jockey Derek Ancil tries to help him through

Ayala (P. Buckley) gets home from Carrickbeg (Mr. J. Lawrence) to win in 1963 after a gruelling struggle

Round the Canal Turn they go during the 1962 race. Merryman II, Ernest, Cannobie Lee and Taxidermist are in the lead

The eventual winner Royal Tan (B. Marshall) almost down at the first in 1954

in the newspapers: 'The connection that has existed between Captain Machell and Mr. Richardson was severed immediately after the Grand National.'

The cause of the row was Reugny's starting price of only 5—1. Apparently Machell had delayed his investment, presumably until he was sure that Reugny was ready and well. Meanwhile 'all Lincolnshire' was on the horse. Richardson lived in Lincolnshire and was popular among the people of town and village. He was stung by Machell's rebuke that he didn't 'keep horses for Lincolnshire farmers to bet on'.

Richardson seems to have been sickened by the acrimony and insulted by Machell's arrogance. He retired from racing to become master of the Brocklesby hounds and to dabble in politics, contesting the Brigg division of Lincolnshire four times.

The year: 1875
Number of runners: Nineteen
Winner: Pathfinder (Mr. Thomas—10 st 11 lb)
Time: 10 minutes 22 seconds

The Grand National prize to the winning owner rose to nearly £2,000 and a contemporary wrote: 'The jumping business, which was once looked on as a mere interlude during the racing recess, has assumed such proportions as almost to menace the position of the sister sport. In former times steeplechasing was confined to a very select few, and those for the most part had no connection with the Turf proper.'

It was a remarkable tribute to the National Hunt Committee, who within ten years had made the sport comparatively 'clean' and respectable.

Pathfinder was a mediocre horse who had raced as The Knight. His dam's pedigree was not known, but his sire was Mogador and his great-grandam Pocahontas. He had changed hands for £100 and was owned in partnership by Lord Huntly, nicknamed 'Cock of the North', and Mr. Herbert Bird in whose name he ran. Tom Pickernell, still officially 'Mr. Thomas', although the pseudonym deceived none, was riding in his eighteenth Grand National.

Captain Machell was represented by Laburnum, a son of King Tom, but Machell's luck was out. Ridden by Jewett following the retirement of Richardson, Laburnum broke a leg and had to be destroyed.

At Becher's for the second time it seemed that the French mare La Venie and Dainty had the race to themselves. Pickernell was so tired that he considered pulling up, but with half a mile remaining Pathfinder surprised everyone by making headway. The French hope dropped out and Dainty was in front at the last hurdle, but Pickernell was restored by the prospect of winning for the third time. He came with a strong run to win by half a length. La Venie was third and Jackal, ridden by Marsh, fourth.

A report said: 'We doubt much if anybody else . . . could have won on Pathfinder. After riding eighteen years "Mr. Thomas" has shown us that though the years have crept on since he won on Anatis, his nerve and judgment were never better.'

There was a change of mind among the connections of the second horse, Dainty. An objection to the winner was lodged, then withdrawn before it could be considered.

The year: 1876
Number of runners: Nineteen
Winner: Regal (J. Cannon—11 st 3 lb)
Time: 11 minutes 14 seconds

Captain Machell became the first owner since horse-dealer John Elmore to win the National three times. He did it with Regal at 25—1 to the dismay of those who had helped to make his other entry, Chandos, a 100—30 favourite.

Defence had been sold to Mr. Hector Baltazzi, who raced in France as well as in England and whose brother owned the Derby winner Kisber. Pickernell rode Defence, while the 1875 winner, Pathfinder, making his last appearance in a National, was ridden by his Epsom trainer, W. Reeves.

The black Chimney Sweep, a former charger in the cavalry, set a bold gallop from Master Mowbray, The Liberator and Shifnal. The Liberator fell at Valentine's, while Zero came down so heavily that his rider, 'Mr. Rolly', was rumoured dead and believed by doctors to have a broken neck. 'Mr. Rolly' refused to believe it and lived to become Lord Minto, Viceroy of India and Governor-General of Canada.

Public hopes crashed with Chandos. The best-looking steeplechaser for several years, he had finished fourth in the Derby and was said to be Captain Machell's favourite horse. A commentator wrote: 'The confidence of Captain Machell in Chandos was something sublime.' But Machell took no chances on the day, coupling his bets with Regal.

It was a close finish. Joe Cannon had Regal on one side of the course, Mr. E. P. Wilson had Congress on the other. A dead-heat seemed probable as horses and riders fought out the last strides, but Cannon drove Regal to win by a neck. It was perhaps a lucky win, for Mr. Wilson, who would ride the winners in 1884 and 1885, thought Congress had been hindered crucially by loose horses. A report sustains that opinion with the comment: 'We must class him [Captain Machell] with Lord Rosebery as one of the most fortunate men of the day.'

There was no quarrel between owner and jockey this time. Regal's price was five times that of Reugny and slightly longer than the 20—1 against Disturbance in 1873.

Shifnal was third, ridden by I'Anson. Chimney Sweep finished. So did Rye, Jackal and Master Mowbray.

The year: 1877
Number of runners: Sixteen
Winner: Austerlitz (Mr. E. C. Hobson—10st 8lb)
Time: 10 minutes 16 seconds

To win the National became the ambition of more and more members of the House of Lords. Lord Lonsdale bought Regal and Congress for a double-barrelled attempt, hoping that his son would ride Congress. But an injury sustained in another race spoiled that intent, and Joe Cannon, brilliantly successful on Regal the previous year, was engaged. Jewett rode Regal and there was plenty of support for Reugny, the winner in 1874.

Chimney Sweep and Shifnal were back again, while newcomer Austerlitz, five years old and handicapped at 10 st 8 lb, might have found greater support had he been ridden by a professional. His amateur rider, Mr. Hobson, horrified some and amused others by clinging to the cantle of the saddle as Austerlitz jumped each fence. It was the most original way of getting round that students of the race had ever seen. But it succeeded, as more polished styles did not. Austerlitz was not far behind as the leaders reached the hurdles in the straight.

The Liberator led, followed by Chimney Sweep, Shifnal, Dainty and Congress. Pickernell stole a length on The Liberator and seemed likely to win until gallant Congress came at him, not yielding an inch. They fought each other to a standstill, then had nothing left when Hobson arrived. Austerlitz swept past both to win by four lengths from Congress. The Liberator was third.

Arthur Yates, the steeplechase jockey who became a successful trainer, suggested later that Mr. Hobson was underestimated because of his style. His clinging to the saddle was not caused by fear, only by a theory that it took some strain off the horse's shoulders and shifted the rider's weight as far back as possible. Mr. Hobson did not ride in another National, although he won at other meetings.

Some records attribute the ownership of Austerlitz to him, which would make him the first owner since Alan McDonough in 1838 to ride his own winner. Other sources name 'Mr. F. Hobson' as the owner.

Austerlitz was entered the following year, but did not run. On the eve of the race he was found to be 'wrong' in a leg and was withdrawn.

The year: 1878
Number of runners: Twelve
Winner: Shifnal (J. Jones—10 st 12 lb)
Time: 10 minutes 23 seconds

The afternoon began with a fright, when smoke billowed beneath the royal box erected for the Prince of Wales. Loose straw was found to be on fire and the panic was more dangerous than the blaze.

It was to prove a race of ironies for Yorkshireman I'Anson. Narrowly beaten on Scarrington in 1872, he had subsequently ridden Shifnal without much success and thought the old horse, owned by John Nightingall of Epsom, could not have improved with years. I'Anson preferred His Lordship, the favourite. Jack Jones took the ride on Shifnal, while the Irish were represented by the mares Martha, ridden by Tom Beasley, and Pride of Kildare ridden by G. Moore. Captain Machell had bought Jackal in an attempt to win a fourth National.

The field was small and accidents were few, although His Lordship and The Bear were brought down. Martha was an early leader from Miss Lizzie, but towards the end of the second circuit Jackal, Pride of Kildare and Shifnal began to improve. Martha was spent when Shifnal, shrugging off Jackal and Pride of Kildare, challenged on the flat to win by two lengths.

Pride of Kildare was third with Jackal fourth. Miss Lizzie, Curator and Boyne got round, which meant that more than half the field were standing at the finish.

Shifnal and Jones had waited a long time for their triumph. Shifnal had finished third and sixth, while Jones had been fourth twice, fifth and second and had never fallen. They had to wait further minutes before their triumph was confirmed, for Tom Beasley lodged an official protest, accusing Jones of foul riding. The objection was quickly overruled and left a bitter taste. It was the first time a formal objection had been heard against a winner of the National.

The year: 1879
Number of runners: Eighteen
Winner: The Liberator (G. Moore—11 st 4 lb)
Time: 10 minutes 12 seconds

Four brothers weighed out for this race. They were the Beasleys, led by Tom who had finished second on Martha the previous year. He was engaged to ride the mare again, while his brother Willie rode Lord Marcus, Harry rode Turco and John rode Victor II.

Another Irishman, Garrett Moore, rode his own horse, The Liberator. Both were experienced over Aintree fences, but only the Irish thought The Liberator might emulate Shifnal and win after repeated failures. They backed him down to 5—1, unaware that shortly before the race he had pulled up lame from a morning gallop.

Tom Beasley repeated his runaway tactics on Martha, but the mare had little left when challenged by Jackal, destined never to win, yet fourth twice and sixth in previous years and outpaced now by The Liberator. Ridden on a long rein by Moore, who became the second owner-rider to succeed, The Liberator won in a canter.

Jackal was second, beaten ten lengths, and Martha third. Wild Monarch, Bob Ridley, Regal and Rossanmore finished, while two other Beasley brothers survived their first look at Aintree fences by getting Lord Marcus and Turco round.

The decade dominated by Captain Machell was over. Another, dominated by an Irishman who built duplicates of Aintree fences and who made winning the National his governing purpose, was about to begin.

7

The Irishman was H. E. Linde, of Eyrefield Lodge, who built duplicates of Aintree fences at his Curragh training grounds, thereby ensuring that young horses came to Aintree thoroughly schooled. But Linde had more than good horses. He had the men to ride them; including the Beasley brothers, of whom Tom and Harry were to ride four National winners between 1880 and 1891. Moreover he had owners who could afford patient preparation, always with the National as the objective.

They were professionals, skilful and patient and shrewd. Their success was such that an English magazine complained: 'We have beyond all doubt lost the supremacy in the rearing and production of cross-country performers.' It was an allegation which English breeders and trainers would soon refute, but in the early 1880s any Linde-trained horse was worth support and got it.

The year: 1880
Number of runners: Fourteen
Winner: Empress (T. Beasley—10 st 7 lb)

Empress was named as a compliment to the Empress of Austria, who frequently visited Linde at Eyrefield Lodge during hunting holidays in Ireland. He bought the big chestnut as a three-year-old, racing her mildly on the flat but schooling her vigorously at home. He believed that steeplechasers should be jumped often 'to get their jumping muscles up'. At five years old, when she came to Aintree in the colours of Mr. P. Ducrot, she was presumed a total novice only by those who didn't know about the rigorous preparation on the Curragh.

Regal was made favourite, with the 1879 winner, The Liberator, backed to win again at eleven years old. The French challenge was represented by Wild Monarch, ridden by I'Anson. Empress was ridden by Tom Beasley and heavily backed by the Irish at 8—1. Harry Beasley rode Woodbrook, John rode Victoria. The race was a Royal occasion, attended by the Prince of Wales and watched by a crowd so large it was estimated to be another record.

There was a howl of dismay as Regal fell at 'Fan's Fence'. Wild Monarch, Shifnal and Downpatrick made the running on the first circuit, but as they turned towards the country for the second time Mr. Lee Barber sent his own horse, Jupiter Tonans, to the front at what was described as 'flat-race speed'. At one stage he was a furlong in front, but the bookmakers weren't impressed. They still offered 50—1 against.

Jupiter Tonans began to falter and Downpatrick seemed to have a chance. But Beasley brought Empress through the stragglers to pass Downpatrick after Valentine's. In the closing stages the race was between Empress and The Liberator, who was giving weight as well as six years. The Liberator was a good horse, but he could not hold off the 'flying mare'.

Empress saved her best leap to the last and ran on to win by two lengths. Downpatrick was a close third, while Jupiter Tonans struggled into the picture to finish fourth, raising speculation about what might have happened if Mr. Lee Barber had ridden a more cautious race. There was criticism also of Garrett Moore, who was accused of failing to get the most out of The Liberator in the final duel. Cynics noted that Moore had a close association with Eyrefield Lodge.

Woodbrook, Wild Monarch, Victor II, Victoria, Shifnal and

Dainty were still there at the finish. In a field of fourteen, only four failed to get round.

The Irish went home in merry mood, sure that this was only the first of several Nationals which Empress could win. But the five-year-old never ran again. Her legs were so shaken by rigorous training that she was sent to stud. Such premature retirement was the first of several comments on Linde's methods.

The year: 1881
Number of runners: Thirteen
Winner: Woodbrook (T. Beasley—11st 3lb)
Time: 11 minutes 50 seconds

For the third time the number of runners was considered ominous and for the first time it snowed as well as rained throughout the week. The going was a quagmire. Horses floundered in the mangold fields. Some could not go beyond a trot. It was a day made for Woodbrook, fifth the previous year and a known mudlark.

Only The Liberator, carrying 12 st 7 lb and conceding as much as 35 lb to the bottom weights, could keep with him for a time. But the twelve-year-old fell at Valentine's and the challenge was left to another veteran, Regal, the winner in 1876 but disappointing since. Regal fought bravely to the last hurdle, where Woodbrook drew away to win in a canter by four lengths. Thornfield, a natural jumper who had failed on the flat, was third. The Scot, owned by Captain Machell, was ridden by the ex-flat-race jockey, Fred Webb. Others to finish were New Glasgow, Abbott of St. Mary's, Cross Question, Montauban, and finally the remounted Liberator who, with great courtesy, had made no attempt to get away from Moore after the fall at Valentine's.

It was another triumph for Tom Beasley. In four years he had ridden second and third and had won the National twice.

Colonel Tom Kirkwood, of Co. Roscommon, sold Woodbrook for £1,300 to the German, Herr Ochlschlaeger. The price seemed cheap but again the racing career of a Linde-trained horse was nearly over. Woodbrook died the following year at Newmarket.

The year: 1882
Number of runners: Twelve
Winner: Seaman (Lord Manners—11 st 6 lb)
Time: 10 minutes 42$\frac{3}{5}$ seconds

It could have been a hat-trick for the Eyrefield Lodge combination of Linde-Beasley, but for once Linde's judgment erred. He had in his yard a brilliant young horse, Seaman, winner of the Conyngham Cup at Punchestown as well as of the Paris Hurdle in France. But Seaman developed a suspect leg and Linde persuaded John Gubbins to sell. Lord Manners, a young Guards officer, bought him for £2,000, apparently unaware of what all Ireland knew.

Lord Manners sent Seaman to be trained at Newmarket by James Jewett and declared his intention to ride in the National. Local opinion was that he'd been out-smarted in Ireland and that the horse had 'no chance'. *Bell's Life* commented: 'Seaman has no friends now at any price.'

The Irish challenge was led by Cyrus, trained by Linde and ridden by Tom Beasley. It seemed an invincible combination, although pre-race trials suggested that Linde's other runner, Mohican, might steal the race. For this reason and with Linde's encouragement, Mohican was made favourite.

Again snow froze in the faces of the crowds. Again the going was 'more an Irish bog', but this time there was no Woodbrook to celebrate it. The running was made by Wild Monarch, now in English ownership, and after Becher's by the Duke of Hamilton's Eau de Vie, ridden by Dan Thirlwell. Reports suggest that Thirlwell was unlucky. He kept the lead until Becher's on the second circuit, where he pulled up with a broken stirrup.

For the first time in several years there was tragic accident when Wild Monarch, tiring in the mud, fell and broke a leg. The Liberator, Fay, The Scot and Linde's professed preference, Mohican, were other fallers, leaving Captain Smith on Zoedone in front. For a while the five-year-old mare promised to beat the Irish at last, but Beasley brought Cyrus with a devastating burst, seeming to have the race won as they reached the hurdles.

It was then the astonished crowd became aware of Seaman, still coming despite his suspect leg and despite the inexperience of his rider. *Bell's Life* reported: 'From the last hurdle, which he jumped a little sideways, Seaman had a length to make up, and with Lord Manners against Tommy Beasley, it was apparently a one-sided duel. To the intense astonishment of those who had been prejudiced against him, Lord Manners finished in a workmanlike manner. . . .'

Apparently Beasley was incredulous. The same report reproached him for riding 'in hustled manner, which suggested he had been caught unawares'. *Bell's Life* spoke for England when it laughed: 'It must have been gall and wormwood to the Linde division to have been beaten by one of their own cast-offs.'

It was more than that. It was victory for the 'Mug' over the horse-trader; for the titled amateur over the professional. It was a fairy-tale victory and the cheers which greeted Lord Manners, the first peer to ride the winner, were the loudest the Liverpool sky had ever heard.

But the cheers faded as the crowds saw what had happened to the horse. Seaman was lame. His hind leg had finally broken down, probably at the last hurdle where he had jumped 'a little sideways'. Immediate retirement was imperative. Seaman never raced again, while his owner never rode again in a National.

It might have been coincidence that three Linde-schooled winners in succession were as good as finished when their race was won. But English trainers, at the time and since, thought premature break-down a comment on Linde's methods. What happened to Empress, Woodbrook and Seaman, none of them over seven and not yet in their steeplechasing prime, confirmed the belief that excessive schooling over big obstacles placed too great a strain on young legs.

The year: 1883
Number of runners: Ten
Winner: Zoedone (Count C. Kinsky—11 st)
Time: 11 minutes 39 seconds

These were boom years for steeplechasing, yet the average field for the National in the 1880s was only sixteen, four less than in the previous decade. This might have been because the standard of competition was rising, so that owners were discouraged from sending forlorn hopes. But a sub-committee, appointed by the National Hunt Committee to report on the decline, expressed the opinion that reduction in the size and variety of fences had so changed the sport that steeplechasing 'which fifty years ago was all jumping is now all galloping'. In addition, owners of National horses had complained for years about the futility of 'small, trappy fences' at Aintree and about the hazards caused by crowds encroaching on the course.

The National Hunt Committee had urged the Aintree administration to maintain fences at a proper standard, but changes were slow. Although the fences were improved in 1883, part of the course continued to be plough and not all of it was railed in.

The going was again heavy from persistent rain. The Linde-trained Zitella, ridden by Tom Beasley, was made favourite, with Eau de Vie, Montauban, Downpatrick and Black Prince among the fancied. The Linde stable was also represented by last year's failure, Mohican, ridden by Harry Beasley.

During the morning there was increasing support for Zoedone, ridden by his owner, Count Kinsky, a Hungarian friend of the Empress of Austria in whose honour the winner in 1880 had been named. Count Kinsky had bought the six-year-old mare from Mr. Clayton shortly before the race, using £800 won on the Cesarewitch and promising to pay £200 more if she won the National. Mr. Clayton must have considered it a generous price, for although Zoedone had won two minor steeplechases at the age of four and was a safe jumper, she lacked finishing speed. To date her third in the National of 1882 was her only claim to serious attention.

But Count Kinsky applied himself to the business of winning, training like an athlete while Upton trainer, W. Jenkins, prepared the horse. Both came to Aintree fit and ready. Count Kinsky's luck was twofold: first that the higher fences favoured Zoedone at the expense of faster horses, second that the deep going made stamina more important than speed.

Mohican failed again and *Bell's Life*, describing both Mohican and Zitella as 'over-done', complained that Zitella could not be recognised as the 'mare that had run at Kempton in February, all the nature having been taken out of her'. It was a scathing indictment of Linde and his reputation was never quite so high again.

Black Prince, ridden by Canavan, tried to narrow the gap when Zoedone flew Valentine's on the second circuit. But Count Kinsky was already on his way into history as the last owner-rider to succeed in the National. He had six lengths in hand over Black Prince at the finish. Zitella was third, Downpatrick fourth. Montauban and Eau de Vie were far behind.

For the second year an amateur had defeated professionals, but the time of eleven minutes thirty-nine seconds was considerably slower than Seaman's and no less than ninety-four seconds slower than the winner the following year.

The year: 1884
Number of runners: Fifteen
Winner: Voluptuary (Mr. E. P. Wilson—10 st 5 lb)
Time: 10 minutes 5 seconds

Voluptuary's qualifications were two hurdle races. Like Alcibiade in 1865, he had never jumped a fence in public, although he'd been hunted in Warwickshire so regularly that it was said he had 'jumped every fence in the county'.

Bred at the Hampton Court stud and originally owned by

Queen Victoria, he was sold to Lord Rosebery for 660 guineas as a yearling. He ran without much distinction on the flat, including the Derby of 1881. At five years old he was sold at Newmarket sales to Mr. H. F. Boyd for 150 guineas, a bargain price for one of the best bred horses ever to win a National.

By Cremorne out of Miss Evelyn, Voluptuary was ridden by E. P. Wilson, the rider of Montauban in 1883. The schooling was long and patient, and Wilson came to Aintree certain that Voluptuary was the best horse in the race.

This was no small boast for the field included Zoedone, Roquefort, Zitella, Satellite and Frigate. Poor old Regal, the winner as long ago as 1876, was also there, but his legs were described as 'dreadful'. It could have surprised none when he dropped from a gallop to a painful stumble, so lame that not even an ambitious owner, seeking a place among the privileged rather than hoping to win, could ask him to try again.

The Scot ran well for his new owner, the Prince of Wales, whose colours appeared in a National for the first time. Jack Jones, recommended by Lord Marcus Beresford, was the Royal jockey. But his luck ran out at Becher's second time round. The Scot straddled the fence and although he got over, his chance was gone.

Zoedone led from Roquefort and Frigate as they approached the final hurdles, but the winner of 1883 had 12 st 2 lb to carry. She had never had many pretensions to speed and the additional weight, plus the faster pace, put her out of it when Roquefort, Frigate and Voluptuary battled to the last hurdle. Harry Beasley drove Frigate to the front and might have won if the six-year-old, destined to compete in seven Nationals and to wait a long time for victory, had not stumbled on landing. Voluptuary jumped it smoothly and showed Derby-class speed on the flat to win by four lengths.

Frigate was second and Roquefort third, followed by Zoedone, Cyrus and Black Prince. It was said of Roquefort that he had once pulled a dog-cart. Arthur Yates saw him in a sale of harness horses, recognised his potential and schooled him at Arlesford Downs. His performance in the National on that 'Royal day', when the horses passed in and out of the mist like horses in a dream, so impressed Wilson on the winner that he persuaded Mr. Arthur Cooper to buy. The way was open for a remarkable double.

The year: 1885
Number of runners: Nineteen
Winner: Roquefort (Mr. E. P. Wilson—11 st)
Time: 10 minutes 10 seconds

The race was run entirely on grass and for the first time the whole of the course was railed in. These improvements, however belated, encouraged the biggest field since 1876, with the six-year-old Roquefort a hot favourite at 100—30. He was receiving 10 lb from Frigate, while the consistent Zoedone had the top weight of 11 st 11 lb.

Despite this burden Zoedone had been coupled in doubles with Bendigo, winner of the Lincolnshire Handicap, and bookmakers stood to lose heavily if the mare won. In some way, never discovered despite investigation and speculation, Zoedone was 'stopped' between her arrival at Aintree and leaving the paddock.

In those days it was still obligatory to jump a preliminary hurdle on the way to the start. Zoedone was seen to be bleeding from the nose as she began to canter. She reached the hurdle and seemed about to jump with her usual skill. But she only half-rose to it and fell awkwardly. Count Kinsky was shaken, as much mentally as physically for his favourite mare had never before made such a blunder. He remounted and took her to the start, soothing her all the time, apparently unable to believe that she could be the victim of conspiracy.

She completed the first circuit 'like a dead thing', seeming to be jumping from memory, merely following others without her usual zest for racing. Somehow she got round to Becher's for the second time, where she took off in a way never forgotten by those who saw. She was famed for the generosity of her jumping, but this time the leap was not upward and forward. It was vertical, a kind of convulsive contortion like the death-throes of a deer. She crashed down and writhed, her legs threshing in such pain that an angry crowd pressed closer. Count Kinsky stood beside her, his heart-break showing in his face. An old woman said afterwards, 'None of us will forget the way he looked, for everyone knew how he loved that mare.'

A veterinary surgeon subsequently reported that Zoedone had been poisoned. She never raced again, but some good came out of the tragedy. Other owners and trainers were made sharply aware of the need for closer security, for a weeding out of the disreputable from racecourse stables.

The race continued in anticlimax. Roquefort, still pulling Wilson's arms out and looking for a chance to quit, won by two lengths from Frigate, so that Wilson's triumph over Harry Beasley was repeated. Black Prince, second and sixth in previous years, was third, followed by Redpath, Axminster, Albert Cecil and Dog Fox. Last to finish was Lioness, ridden by Mr. George Lambton.

Wilson became the fifth rider to win in successive years. He'd begun his Aintree career with Congress in 1873 and had been beaten only narrowly by Joe Cannon on Regal in 1876. When he gave up riding in 1898, he'd been on the steeplechase scene for nearly thirty-five years. His style was unusual, in that he favoured short leathers and short reins. It was most effective with sluggish jumpers or with wilful horses. Perhaps no other of the decade could have ridden Roquefort so successfully, for the hard-puller was also sly, always waiting for some hint of relaxation so that he could run out.

The year: 1886
Number of runners: Twenty-three
Winner: Old Joe (T. Skelton—10 st 9 lb)
Time: 10 minutes 14⅗ seconds

The biggest field since 1873 included a harness horse, bred in Cumberland, named after a huntsman and ridden by a tough cross-country jockey who had waited a long time for a change of luck.

The horse was Old Joe, named after Joe Graham, huntsman to the Dumfriesshire. Joe bought the horse for £30 from his breeder, Mr. Briscoe, then sold him to Mr. A. J. Douglas, who found that his humble purchase was something more than a safe ride to hounds. Old Joe had the fighting qualities essential to a National winner.

Linde was represented by Too Good, owned by Count Erdody but known to have a 'doubtful' leg. Coronet was favourite, partly because rider Wilson was trying for a hat-trick. The Liberator was making a last appearance, while Cortolvin, ridden by Dollery and owned by Abingdon Baird, had borrowed the name of the 1867 winner. Black Prince was there again and George Lambton was riding Redpath.

The increase in the number of runners meant a scramble for the first fence. Frigate came down, leaving Old Joe in front, followed by Roquefort and Gamecock. At the end of the first circuit Coronet quickened the pace from Savoyard, Lady Tempest and Gamecock. They were followed by Too Good and the unconsidered horse from Cumberland who had jumped in agricultural shows.

Coronet faded and Savoyard fell at the last. Suddenly Old Joe, ridden by Tom Skelton, was in front and full of fight. Linde's Too Good wasn't good enough, while Gamecock ran bravely to finish third.

The luck had suddenly changed for Skelton. He proved lucky in his owner also, for Mr. Douglas gave him the prize money of £1,300.

The year: 1887
Number of runners: Sixteen
Winner: Gamecock (W. Daniells—11 st)
Time: 10 minutes 10⅕ seconds

Some horses win the National at the first attempt, then spend years trying to repeat the feat. Others wait for the luck which every winner needs. Such a one was Gamecock, locally owned, trained by Jordan and a hot tip on Merseyside at 20—1.

Old Joe was back after running in the Cesarewitch where he was beaten by 'about half a mile'. His rider was Mr. C. J. Cunningham, Skelton getting the ride on the strongly fancied Savoyard, half-brother to Zoedone and thought unlucky in 1886. But the pre-race gossip was all for Spahi, trained by Linde for John Gubbins; a whirlwind winner on the flat but untried in public over fences or hurdles. Two days before the race a journalist quoted an Irish friend: 'I never remember so great a steeplechasing certainty. . . . He can stay for a month and is a faultless jumper.'

Too Good was another Irish representative, while Sam Darling, later to train Derby winners, sent a pony-sized steeplechaser called Ballot Box, owned by Sir Patterson Nickalls and originally trained by him 'round my cabbage garden'. Roquefort and Frigate were Aintree veterans and George Lambton rode his own mare, Bellona.

The race began with disaster for the Irish. Spahi fell at the third, although how good a horse he was may be judged by the fact that the following day he ran on the flat over two miles to be narrowly beaten by Bird of Freedom, winner of the Ascot Gold Cup three months later.

Ballot Box was another early faller and as they approached the end, the old names had it to themselves. Roquefort, Frigate, Old Joe and Savoyard came over Valentine's as though in answer to a roll-call of 'Aintree regulars'. Roquefort suddenly got the better of Wilson, swerving wildly and crashing through the rails. Savoyard took up the running, giving Skelton hopes of another victory. But the local cheers were for Gamecock, still making progress, his head so low he seemed to be going into each fence 'like a ratting terrier'.

Gamecock jumped the last in front and pulled away to win by three lengths from Savoyard. Johnny Longtail, owned by Lord Wolverton and ridden by Childs, made up ground from the last to finish third.

The year: 1888
Number of runners: Twenty
Winner: Playfair (Mawson—10 st 7 lb)
Time: 10 minutes 12 seconds

The course was altered to its final shape, finishing over two small fences within the flat-race course. Spahi, the fallen 'certainty' of 1887, became a 33—1 chance. The new favourite was from the same stable and in the same ownership; Usna, unbeaten and carrying 12 st 7 lb, giving 3lb to Gamecock and Savoyard. Walter Nightingall, offered a choice, preferred tiny Ballot Box to the novice Playfair, whose only claim was a hurdle success at Sandown. An unknown jockey, Mawson, took the ride.

It was an eventful afternoon for Mawson. He seemed to have no chance on the second circuit when Playfair straddled a fence and had him clinging cowboy-fashion. He would have fallen if Arthur Nightingall, riding close on The Badger, had not reached for him and pulled him back in one of those gestures for which steeplechasing is happily renowned. Mawson had scarcely recovered saddle and stirrups when Frigate dashed across him to avoid the fallen Usna. His hopes seemed faint as he settled down to ride in pursuit of Skelton on Ringlet.

Ringlet faded and Savoyard fell at the first of the new fences. Frigate went on an apparent winner, but Mawson, having survived so much, would not be denied. He forced Playfair in front and held on by ten lengths, with Sam Darling's Ballot Box a commendable third. Gamecock got round again, accompanied by Aladdin, Jeamie and The Badger.

The year: 1889
Number of runners: Twenty
Winner: Frigate (T. Beasley—11 st 4 lb)
Time: 10 minutes $1\frac{1}{5}$ seconds

Frigate began the day as one of the unluckiest horses in Aintree history; three times second in 1884, 1885 and 1888, when ridden by Harry or Willie Beasley. Owner-breeder Mr. M. A. Maher, who had sold her once, then bought her back, believed she was better than Empress and in *A Hundred Grand Nationals* T. H. Bird described her as 'the best mare that has ever won the Grand National'. What happened to the daughter of Gun Boat that afternoon was to delight the crowd and persuade future owners and trainers that persistence can change the luck.

Voluptuary and Roquefort were back. So was Savoyard, ridden by Lambton. The Prince of Wales ran Magic and Hettie, while promising newcomers were Why Not and M.P. Despite his spectacular run-out in 1887, Roquefort was favourite in a moderate field.

This was Frigate's first bit of luck, since in other years she had always found one too good. Her second bit of luck was the sudden departure of the Hungarian entry, Et Coetera, owned by Count Nicholas Esterhazy and reputedly a faultless jumper. The Hungarian crashed at the third. Voluptuary fell when going strongly from M.P. and Why Not. Roquefort was another faller, leaving Why Not in front, followed by The Fawn and M.P.

Two from home Why Not was clear, but Tommy Beasley, with his third National in sight, kept old Frigate pounding towards cheers so loud and sustained that those too far away to see thought a Royal horse had won. Frigate had a length in hand from Why Not. M.P. was third, followed by Bellona, Magic, The Sikh, The Fawn, Ringlet, Battle Royal and Gamecock.

'The year Frigate won' was a milestone in the history of the race. Sensible compromise had come out of muddled criticism and derision. Fences were not as formidable as the owners of reliable hunter-types might have hoped, but they were no longer 'small and trappy'. The course was railed in and the distance was established at four and a half miles. Moreover the weight-range, for so long the cause of bitter controversy, was much less eccentric. In the 1890s only one light-weight was to win, while two were to succeed with the burden of 12 st 7 lb.

8

The year: 1890
Number of runners: Sixteen
Winner: Ilex (A. Nightingall—10 st 5 lb)
Time: 10 minutes $41\frac{4}{5}$ seconds

Ilex was a hunter chaser, a winner over two miles at Leicester where he had been bought in for 250 guineas. Mr. H. R. Singleton had sold him to Mr. G. Masterman, a remarkable owner in that he betted heavily yet liked others to bet with him. With Arthur Nightingall engaged to ride, Mr. Masterman announced to all who cared to listen that Ilex was 'an absolute certainty bar accidents'.

Paddock judges thought otherwise. The horse seemed 'all barrel and no bone', short in the shoulders and 'wrong in the back'. They doubted that trainer John Nightingall could have done much with him and preferred veterans Frigate, Voluptuary and Gamecock, all beyond their best but known to jump and stay. Others in the field were M.P., a promising third the previous year, Why Not, Bellona, Hetty and Battle Royal. There was also Pan, 100—1 against and known to be a rogue.

Why Not fell early; poor Frigate slipped at the fence before Valentine's; Voluptuary came down at the last open ditch and jockey Skelton broke a collar-bone. Gamecock made a rare mistake. One by one the old campaigners eliminated themselves, so that as they approached the straight Ilex had only M.P. to beat. He did it with ease, then held off a surprising challenge from the rogue Pan to win by ten lengths.

M.P. was third for the third successive year, followed by Brunswick, the remounted Why Not, and Emperor. It was a first triumph for Arthur Nightingall and although he rode other National winners in 1894 and 1901, he always described Ilex as the best horse he ever rode.

The year: 1891
Number of runners: Twenty-one
Winner: Come Away (*H. Beasley—11 st 12 lb*)
Time: 9 minutes 58 seconds

For several years the Irish had arrived with hopes and had returned in mourning; but 1891 was to see a revival of their fortunes in Come Away, a powerful bay by Cambuslang, trained as well as ridden by Harry Beasley, although there remained an indirect association with Linde and Eyrefield Lodge. Harry was the only jockey who had ever ridden the seven-year-old. He'd won at Punchestown and a minor race at Liverpool and the Irish backed him to 4—1 favouritism, although he'd had trouble with a suspensory ligament since his four-year-old races.

Ilex was second favourite, with plenty of support for the Linde-trained Cruiser, ridden by Tommy Beasley. Cloister was a newcomer, ridden by Roddy Owen. Voluptuary, Roquefort and Gamecock were trying for the last time.

It was a spectacular race. When they reached the water Cloister, Roquefort and Gamecock were in line and a fast time looked certain. The pace was too much for old Voluptuary. Emperor, owned by Captain Machell, broke his neck. At Valentine's for the second time Roddy Owen had Cloister in front, followed by Ilex, Why Not and Come Away. Why Not fell. Ilex could not stay with them and as they jumped the last, Come Away and Cloister had it between them. Their riders fought a duel reminiscent of Tom Beasley and Jones in 1878, of Tom Beasley and Lord Manners in 1882.

Roddy Owen tried to squeeze between Come Away and the rails, but Beasley shut off the gap. The tactic was probably crucial, for Come Away had only a length in hand at the finish. The angry Owen objected, despite a warning by trainer Marsh: 'You may be second again.' The stewards confirmed the trainer's opinion, overruling the objection.

Ilex was third, followed by Roquefort, Gamecock and Cruiser, on whom Tommy Beasley was having his last National ride.

This Irish triumph cast a sad shadow, for Come Away, having set the fastest time since The Lamb in 1871, pulled up a cripple, that suspensory ligament having collapsed beyond repair. In an attempt to patch him up the horse was fired all round, but his joints were 'twice the ordinary size' and not even Sam Darling, to whom owner Mr. W. C. Jameson sent him, could get him to a racecourse again.

The year: 1892
Number of runners: Twenty-five
Winner: Father O'Flynn (Captain R. Owen—10 st 5 lb)
Time: 9 minutes 48⅕ seconds

It was the biggest field in nineteen years and the winner recorded the fastest time in twenty-one. It became known as 'Owen's year'. Born in Montgomeryshire in 1856, Roddy Owen had begun riding at nineteen and had pledged himself to win a National. Foreign service had kept him off the steeplechasing scene until 1885, when he had begun riding regularly. He had almost won on Cloister in 1891 and must have hoped for the ride in 1892. Hopes were dashed when Cloister was sold to Mr. C. Duff and transferred to Arthur Yates' stable, where Mr. J. C. Dormer was engaged to ride.

Owen's luck did not seem to have changed dramatically when he talked himself into the ride on Father O'Flynn, sold by Lord Cholmondeley to Mr. C. G. Wilson for 470 guineas and notorious for sudden refusals. The little horse, less than 15.3 hands high, had been over-raced as a two-year-old and was supposed to hate racing. The possibility of even a fearless rider getting him round Aintree seemed remote, but Owen took the opportunity with great seriousness, shedding weight on the morning of the race by running from Liverpool to Aintree.

Dense fog obscured the far side of the course, so that the stands could not see what was happening until the leaders approached the end of the first circuit. Cloister was going strongly, followed by Flying Column. Billie Taylor bolted with Harry Beasley, carrying him out of the race and simultaneously out of National records. Cloister continued in the lead until Valentine's, where The Midshipmite headed him. The pace was too fast for the challenger's good and Midshipmite soon fell, leaving Cloister again in front, followed by Flying Column, the Irish horse Ardcarn and by Ilex, going well despite top weight. Meanwhile Captain Owen was persuading Father O'Flynn to face his fences and to jump straight.

When they came out of the fog again Father O'Flynn was still there, chasing Cloister towards the last. It became a fight between two amateurs; the determined Owen and Mr. Dormer, who had secured the ride which the Captain had wanted. Cloister seemed to have enough in hand but Father O'Flynn kept coming, as inspired as his rider who was not content with narrow victory. He drove the seven-year-old on and on until the winning margin was twenty lengths.

Ilex was third and Ardcarn, owned by Colonel Kirkwood and trained by Linde, fourth. They were followed by Flying Column, Hollington and Cruiser.

With his ambition achieved, Owen returned to London. The following Monday he was at the War Office, volunteering for foreign service. He was sent to West Africa, then to India and in 1896 was with Kitchener in Egypt. He died during the Dongola expedition, perhaps of cholera, probably of food poisoning.

The year: 1893
Number of runners: Fifteen
Winner: Cloister (W. Dollery—12 st 7 lb)
Time: 9 minutes 42⅖ seconds

It was a race about which hard-bitten men could become lyrical in the evening of their lives. They liked to boast about it, to exaggerate, to declare they had seen the 'champion of champions'. The horse they talked about was Cloister, the first to win with 12 st 7 lb and in a time so fast that the record-keepers blinked.

A huge horse, sold as backward by Irish dealer Mr. James Daly, he had been in the ownership of several until he passed to Mr. C. Duff, who sent him to Hampshire to be trained by Arthur Yates. He had shown what he could do in 1892, when ridden by an amateur and carrying 12 st 3 lb. Popular opinion was that four more pounds could not stop him. Ridden for the first time by a professional, W. Dollery, he was everyone's choice at 9—2.

The Sporting Life reported: 'Once Cloister went to the front the race to all intents and purposes was a veritable procession.' Why Not, Father O'Flynn and The Midshipmite could not catch him 'as he flew over obstacle after obstacle, "jumping the rest of them silly". A great performance grandly achieved, and rewarded by such a spontaneous burst of enthusiasm as has rarely been heard.'

The official distance was forty lengths in the official time of nine minutes forty-two seconds, more than two minutes faster than Woodbrook in 1881. Aesop was second, ridden by Harry Barker. Why Not was a tired third.

The year: 1894
Number of runners: Fourteen
Winner: Why Not (A. Nightingall—11 st 13 lb)
Time: 9 minutes 45⅖ seconds

It should have been Cloister's year again. The public were sure of it, backing the 'champion of champions' despite a handicap weight of 12 st 12 lb. But behind the scenes there were rumours of lameness accompanied by an ominous lengthening of the odds. Mr. Duff called in detectives, suspecting that as with Zoedone and Miss Mowbray, the rogues had somehow got at his horse. Twice Cloister pulled up lame after schooling at Sandown Park and trainer Yates finally telegraphed the owner that on veterinary advice the horse must be withdrawn.

Mr. Duff remained suspicious of foul play, but on the day before the race Yates wrote to the newspapers, attributing lameness to an injury sustained 'in the National last year, though he did not show it at the time'.

With Cloister scratched the way was open at last for Why Not, a persistent trier and due for a change of luck. Owned by Captain C. Fenwick and ridden by Arthur Nightingall, he won by a length and a half despite a top weight of 11 st 13 lb. Lady Ellen II was second and Wild Man from Borneo third.

The year: 1895
Number of runners: Nineteen
Winner: Wild Man from Borneo (J. Widger—10 st 11 lb)
Time: 10 minutes 32 seconds

Again Cloister was given top weight, again he was backed and again he was withdrawn shortly before the race. He had been transferred from Yates' stable to Harry Escott at Lewes, and seemed well until stumbling during an exercise gallop on the downs. Rumours were immediate that he'd been 'got at', but a veterinary surgeon insisted that the horse was genuinely lame on the near fore.

Aesop was made favourite, chiefly because of his second to Cloister in 1893. Horizon was second favourite because he had beaten Cloister at Sandown. Why Not was 50—1, despite his worthy win of the previous year. There was also a newcomer called Manifesto, ridden by Terry Kavanagh. The Irish horse, Wild Man from Borneo, was again ridden by Joseph Widger, son of the owner and a member of a family of horse-dealers in Waterford.

The race was run in fog so thick that some jockeys did not recognise the fences or understand what was happening as horses fell and struggled up and moped away in search of the paddock. Few spectators could see even the finish, in which Wild Man from Borneo won by less than two lengths from Cathal and Van Der Berg. The newcomer, Manifesto, finished fourth, followed by Leybourne, Father O'Flynn, Lady Pat, Dalkeith, Fin Ma Coul II and Molly Maguire.

The year: 1896
Number of runners: Twenty-eight
Winner: The Soarer (Mr. D. Campbell—9 st 13 lb)
Time: 10 minutes 11$\frac{1}{5}$ seconds

The bottom weight was reduced to 9 st 7 lb and the prize increased from £1,500 to £2,500 plus the total entrance stakes. The highest field since 1873 included Why Not, Father O'Flynn, The Midshipmite, Cathal, Van Der Berg, Manifesto, Biscuit, Barcalwhey and a new horse called The Soarer.

David Campbell, serving with the 9th Lancers, had bought The Soarer while in Ireland and had raced him with fair success over fences. Early in 1896 he had sold him for £600 to Colonel W. Walker (later Lord Wavertree) with the stipulation that he should have the ride in the National. Colonel Walker seems never to have seen his purchase before that day, since he didn't recognise him in the parade and asked which horse it was.

Like Count Kinsky in 1883, David Campbell applied himself seriously to the business of winning. He studied every fence and every yard of the two miles circuit. He showed a military concern for detail and in flat contradiction of popular theory concluded that the middle of the course was the best place to be.

There was confusion at the first fence, too many jockeys looking for the best place to jump. Redhill collided with Manifesto and both came down. This was to be Manifesto's only fall at Aintree. Alpheus, Father O'Flynn and The Midshipmite were prominent until The Midshipmite, once considered by his stable to be superior to Cloister, fell heavily.

Rory O'More led on the second circuit from the venerable Why Not, still partnered by Arthur Nightingall. Waterford took up the running after Becher's, followed by Biscuit and Father O'Flynn, ridden by his new owner, Mr. Grenfell.

Father O'Flynn was baulked at the second last, and the way was open for The Soarer, ridden by Campbell with great dash. The Collins-trained horse was in front for the first time and stayed there, holding off Father O'Flynn by a length and a half. Biscuit was third.

Mr. Campbell gave up steeplechasing shortly afterwards, applied himself to his military career as seriously as he had applied himself to winning the National, and rose to senior command as General Sir David Campbell.

The year: 1897
Number of runners: Twenty-eight
Winner: Manifesto (T. Kavanagh—11 st 3 lb)
Time: 9 minutes 49 seconds

It was the Diamond Jubilee of Queen Victoria. Record crowds packed Aintree and the administration responded by introducing a measure designed to help spectators in the paddock. The names of horses were embroidered on white cloths for easy identification; a measure as simple as it was appreciated and of which showman Lynn would have approved.

The Soarer was back, ridden by David Campbell who had returned from service in India. But popular support was focused on Manifesto, the son of Man O' War; strongly made, with high quarters and long, mulish ears. His rider was Terry Kavanagh, who had first ridden Aintree fences on Spahi and had since been second on Lady Ellen II and fourth on Manifesto and Ardcarn. Kavanagh was the sort of tough customer who didn't argue when told to lose weight. His kind sweated it off by carrying sacks of potatoes, then by sleeping in a manure heap.

Manifesto won in nine minutes forty-nine seconds, seven

seconds slower than Cloister and carrying 18 lb less, although he might have been pressed to a faster time if The Soarer had not fallen and fractured his skull. Filbert was second and Ford of Fyne third, followed by Prince Albert, Lotus Lily, Fairy Queen, Seaport II and Nelly Gray.

Owner Mr. H. W. Dyas must have thought that nothing could prevent Manifesto achieving a string of victories. He was the reigning king of steeplechasers, especially at Aintree where he was judged a stone better than on any other course. But Manifesto, as wilful as his sire, broke from his box at Eveleigh on a wild rampage. Trainer Willie McAuliffe finally tempted him back to his box, but he had damaged a pastern so badly that he could not run in the National of the following year.

The year: 1898
Number of runners: Twenty-five
Winner: Drogheda (J. Gourley—10 st 12 lb)
Time: 9 minutes 43⅘ seconds

Heavy rain, followed by wind-driven snow, made the course a quagmire. In the absence of Manifesto it was a day for surprises and the surprise was a six-year-old by Cherry Ripe, owned by Mr. G. Adams and trained by E. Woods. Drogheda was bred near the Irish town of that name, but the Irish thought little of him at 25—1.

Snow blinded the riders as they turned into the country. The Soarer was trying for the last time after an operation on his head. He had fractured his skull when falling in 1897 and was supposed to have recovered. But something was plainly wrong. He jumped stupidly and finally came down. Ultimately he was retired to Longford, where those who rode him found him 'quite mad', liable to gallop wildly and to jump the smallest fence in nervous desperation as though it were Becher's Brook.

Few recognised the horses or colours as they came out of the snow-screen for the last time. Drogheda seemed to be leading from Cathal, Gauntlet and Filbert, but nobody could be sure until they were over the last and pounding towards the finish.

Drogheda, declared by *The Sporting Life* to be 'one of the most brilliant and genuine 'chasers ever saddled', proved his genuineness that day as Cathal, second to Wild Man From Borneo three years before, tried to get on terms. Drogheda stayed full of running to win by three lengths from Cathal, with Gauntlet four lengths away third and Filbert fourth.

The snow was packed so thick on Gourley as he returned to the paddock that someone called: 'You look like a snowman.' When Gourley had thawed he learned that he would have a pension for life from the grateful owner, Mr. Adams.

The year: 1899
Number of runners: Nineteen
Winner: Manifesto (*G. Williamson—12 st 7 lb*)
Time: 9 minutes 49$\frac{4}{5}$ seconds

Manifesto was back, like a major actor to his favourite stage. Since his last appearance he had been sold by solicitor Mr. Dyas to Mr. J. G. Bulteel for £4,000. Mr. Dyas had also sold Gentle Ida to Mr. Horatio Bottomley for an even larger sum and there were many who judged Gentle Ida the better. So did Mr. Dyas, who refused to believe that any horse in the world could give the mare a stone; which was what the handicapper asked of Manifesto. His weight of 12 st 7 lb was 18 lb higher than in 1897 and only Cloister had ever won with such a burden. The Prince of Wales ran Ambush II, and the French sent over Pistache, five times a winner and ridden by Count de Geloes.

Sheriff Hutton, carrying half the money in Worcestershire, made the early running, followed by Corner and Pistache. Gentle Ida fell at Valentine's, while Pistache went at the Chair, his rider lying with legs drawn up and head in arms as the rest of the field jumped over him. Gentle Ida had struggled up and was galloping riderless beside Manifesto, matching him stride for stride as though trying to prove something to those who considered her superior. Manifesto responded by jumping with an audacity that frightened everyone except jockey Williamson, who knew he had only to sit tight and wait for the winning post.

The crowd roared as Manifesto powered down the opposition to win with ears pricked from Ford of Fyne, receiving 25 lb, and Elliman, receiving 34 lb. His time was only a fraction of a second outside his nine minutes forty-nine seconds in 1897, when he had carried less weight.

Spectators in the paddock 'went mad', struggling to touch him, to steal hairs from mane and tail. Like other great horses, Manifesto was something of an actor. He knew he had won and responded to the adulation. Stirring performances were to come, but not again would he reign over Aintree as undisputed king.

9

The great stimulus which steeplechasing received at the end of the century was the active interest of the Prince of Wales. After several unsuccessful attempts to win the National he bought Ambush II on the recommendation of Mr. George Lushington.

Ambush was a big, powerful bay, sired by Ben Battle, but so backward as a juvenile that his breeder, Mr. W. Ashe, could not get rid of him. This was a turning point in the two-year-old's career.

If Ambush had been sold he would have been raced, probably over-raced in the fashion of the period, so that by the time he was five his legs might have been shattered. But Mr. Ashe, unable to sell at £50 and reluctant to part for less, turned the big horse to grass until he was old enough for hunting. Still no one would buy. Even £40 was considered too much. Finally George Lushington recognised him as the type which the Prince of Wales wanted; safe and courageous, likely to show his best form at Aintree. This opinion was vindicated in 1899, when Ambush, ridden by Algy Anthony, finished seventh. He came back in 1900 to be backed down to 4—1 by a patriotic crowd.

The background to the National of 1900 was the Boer War. Early defeats had turned to victories; jingoism was in fashion; any excuse to wave the flag was enough and the triumph of a Prince who was soon to be King touched off celebrations such as Epsom had never seen on Derby day.

The year: 1900
Number of runners: Sixteen
Winner: Ambush II (A. Anthony—11 st 3 lb)
Time: 10 minutes 1 second

For the first time the horses paraded in numerical order. Manifesto was handicapped at 12 st 13 lb to give no less than 48 lb to the bottom weights, and there were few who did not secretly hope the old fellow would do it. But the popular mood was such that a torrent of red-white-and-blue money made Ambush II a near favourite at 4—1.

The favourite was Hidden Mystery, owned by Colonel T. Gallwey, of Co. Waterford, and trained by Sir Charles Nugent. Hidden Mystery had beaten Manifesto at Sandown.

Covert Hack, stable companion of Ambush, fell at the first. Lightly handicapped Nothing bolted with jockey Hoysted. Hidden Mystery seemed a class above the rest on the first circuit, with the one-paced Barsac taking the lead as they turned into the country for the second time. There luck struck as suddenly as lightning. Covert Hack, running loose, crossed Hidden Mystery and bumped Hugh Nugent from the saddle. Suddenly the race was changed. In one dramatic stroke it was wide open.

Harley kept Barsac in front as they approached Becher's on the second circuit. From that point Beermount's Pride, owned by Mr. George Edwardes, went to the front, followed by Lotus Lily and Ambush. Manifesto began to show for the first time. No horse had ever won with such a weight, but at the Canal there were many who thought Manifesto was going to do it. He headed Beermount's Pride and Lotus Lily, then fought off Barsac as the plodder kept coming. Two fences out Manifesto was in front and the incredible seemed about to happen. But Ambush, receiving 24 lb, saved his best work to the last.

Anthony knew the horse well. In fact it was said that he did everything except sleep in the box. Ambush jumped the last in full stride and began to come away. Manifesto fought back. For a while he held on and for a wonderful moment seemed to be in front. But with a hundred yards to go he was plainly spent and George Williamson did not punish him. Ambush drew away and as Manifesto was eased, Barsac stole second place by a neck with Beermount's Pride fourth.

In 1896 the Prince of Wales had won the Derby with Persimmon. But the scene 'was nothing to that of today'. William Allison wrote that those who saw it would never forget 'their own feelings when the grand old Manifesto made his supreme effort under 12 st 13 lb and up to a hundred yards from the finish looked like getting there'.

The cheers were deafening as the Prince of Wales was escorted to the paddock by Lord Derby and Lord Marcus Beresford. *The Sporting Life* reported a scene 'full of hats wafted lavishly into space'. It was to be a great year for the Prince. His Diamond Jubilee would win the Two Thousand Guineas, the Derby and St. Leger.

The year: 1901
Number of runners: Twenty-four
Winner: Grudon (A. Nightingall—10 st)
Time: 9 minutes 47⅘ seconds

Manifesto was withdrawn. Other top weights dropped out for a variety of reasons until Fanciful, owned by Mr. Tunstall-Moore and ridden by W. Cullen, was the top weight at 11 st 6 lb. Then the weather descended, shutting Aintree in a white coffin. The snow was so deep, the wind so shrill that some jockeys objected to riding in it, but the stewards showed the way by walking part of the course. Wags likened them to Good King Wenceslaus, who 'looked out' on much the same scene and left his footprints for others to follow.

In a mediocre field the popular choices were Barsac, Covert Hack, Drumcree, and the Australian horse Levanter, owned by Major J. D. Edwardes and ridden by Tich Mason. There was also Grudon, whose owner Mr. B. Bletsoe took one look at the snow, then sent a lad to the nearest dairy for two pounds of butter. He smeared it into Grudon's feet to prevent the snow from 'balling'. Probably it made the vital difference.

Covert Hack and Barsac were among the leaders on the first circuit while others fell and floundered. True Blue broke a leg; Zodiac fell so heavily that Banner was stunned. Pawnbroker pulled up. Collgardie gave a 'lift' to Halsey, who had set out on Sapper. The casualties came out of the snow like remnants of an army. But still Grudon, supposedly lazy and a non-trier, kept galloping, followed by Drumcree and Buffalo Bill.

At the last Grudon had only to stand up to win. He jumped it generously and came pounding through the snow to win with ease from gallant Drumcree, who was limping from a twisted plate. Buffalo Bill was third. Other gallant survivors of the 'white National' were Coragh Hill, Covert Hack and Prince Tuscan. Cullen, coming back on Fanciful, described the conditions as 'like trying to find the North Pole without a compass'.

It was Arthur Nightingall's third National win and a joke at the time was that Grudon had run 'like a cat through rain' because he was anxious to get it over.

The year: 1902
Number of runners: Twenty-one
Winner: Shannon Lass (D. Read—10 st 1 lb)
Time: 10 minutes 3 seconds

The Prince of Wales had become King Edward VII and Ambush II could not run because the court was still in mourning for Queen Victoria. But Manifesto was back, fourteen years old, handicapped at 12 st 8 lb and ridden by E. Piggott. There were also two horses of names so similar that confusion was inevitable: Drumcree, second the previous year and owned by Mr. J. S. Morrison; and Drumree, owned by the Duke of Westminster and receiving 18 lb from Manifesto.

Heavy rain caused minor accidents. Fairland slipped at the fourth fence, bringing down Drumree. Matthew, ridden by Willie Morgan, was prominent followed by Barsac, Inquisitor, Aunt May, Arnold and Manifesto. But in going so deep, with mud flying back from hooves and splashing the jockeys' faces like brown rain, the top weights were made to feel every pound.

Three fences out Shannon Lass, bred by Mr. H. S. Croker in Co. Limerick and owned by Mr. A. Gorham, began to make rapid progress. Manifesto saw the threat and responded. At the last the crowds were shouting for Matthew and Shannon Lass, with another incredulous and growing cry for Manifesto, giving Shannon Lass 35 lb yet still coming like a champion. It couldn't be done. Everyone knew it. Yet for about fifty strides the old champion looked capable of taking the crown for the third time.

The run-in was too long, the gallop too strong, the mud too deep. He had only courage left and tried to make that enough. The cheers of encouragement became cheers of another kind as Manifesto was seen to be toiling.

Shannon Lass became the eleventh mare to win and the last for more than forty years. Matthew was second, beaten three lengths, with Manifesto three lengths away third.

The year: 1903
Number of runners: Twenty-three
Winner: Drumcree (P. Woodland—11 st 3 lb)
Time: 10 minutes 0⅖ second

King Edward VII came back to Aintree to watch Ambush II try again. It was a great social occasion, for the previous evening Liverpool had given civic welcome to General Baden-Powell. Another hero of the Boer War, Lord Roberts, was among the guests in the paddock.

Ambush had 12 st 7 lb and was handicapped to give 4 lb to Manifesto, partnered again by Williamson and backed by the faithful at 25—1. Percy Woodland was offered the ride on Drumcree, following an injury to Hugh Nugent. Atty Persse weighed out for Marpessa, J. W. Widger for Matthew. The big field included old-timers Fanciful, Inquisitor, Aunt May, Fairland and Pawnbroker as well as newcomers Patlander, Benvenir, Kirkland, and Pride of Mabestown.

Kilmallog broke a leg; Marpessa blundered; Matthew fell when in front; Detail came down as he challenged Drumree after Becher's on the second circuit. Ambush drew away from

Manifesto and chased Drumree towards the last.

Suddenly the Duke of Westminster's horse staggered and stopped, then fell as though shot. It looked all over bar the shouting for Ambush, but the King's horse hit the last and toppled. The way was open for lucky Drumcree to win by ten lengths from Detail. There was another race for third place, Manifesto holding off Kirkland by a head to be accorded more cheers than the 13—2 winner. Others to get round were Fanciful, Pawnbroker and Benvenir.

Meanwhile Drumree was being persuaded to his feet. The horse ambulance stood by, but he could walk and seemed unharmed. Fifty-three years later there would be a similar incident, equally inexplicable, depriving a popular Royal patron of apparently certain victory.

The year: 1904
Number of runners: Twenty-six
Winner: Moifaa (A. Birch—10 st 7 lb)
Time: 9 minutes 59 seconds

King Edward VII was there again, accompanied by Lord Derby. Manifesto was there, too, sixteen years old and giving weight to all except Ambush II; but the parade was dominated physically by Moifaa, a massive horse from New Zealand, more than 17 hands high, a winner over fences in his native country and brought to England by Mr. Spencer Gollans.

Trained by Hickey, the eight-year-old was said to have 'the head and shoulders of a camel'. Paddock judges were fascinated by the ugliness. Everything was 'wrong' because it was excessive, yet in this freak the excessive clicked and on this day nothing could live with him.

Jockey Birch, less pilot than passenger, sat tight and hoped for luck as Moifaa led from the start, headed once by Kirkland but only briefly. Behind him the fancied horses fell like beginners. Ambush fell at the third. Detail came down. So did Patlander, Pride of Mabestown, Comfit, Kiora, Knight of St. Patrick, Deerslayer and Inquisitor, whose sight had been allegedly improved by an operation. Loch Lomond was killed.

Nothing could get near Moifaa as he pounded away to win by eight lengths from Kirkland and The Gunner. Shawn Aboo, a 100—1 chance, was fourth, followed by Robin Hood IV, Band of Hope, Napillah and Manifesto.

It was the last National for Manifesto and Ambush. Lord Marcus Beresford bought Moifaa on behalf of King Edward, but the giant went wrong in his wind, a common affliction among big horses. After a second run at Aintree he was given away as a hunter.

The year: 1905
Number of runners: Twenty-five
Winner: Kirkland (F. Mason—11 st 5 lb)
Time: 9 minutes 48⅕ seconds

Mr. F. Bibby, of Liverpool, shared a financial interest with Mr. L. Phillips in the Irish-bred Kirkland, who had tried to take on Moifaa the previous year and had held on bravely to finish second. A big and genuine stayer he gave Tich Mason his only winning ride in a National.

First past the post was Ascetic's Silver, but he'd left his jockey at the third. Shrewd judges were impressed by his jumping as he continued riderless, followed by Kirkland, Napper Tandy and the pony-size Buckaway II, ridden by A. Newey.

The favourite Moifaa, carrying the Royal colours, had disappeared at Becher's.

The year: 1906
Number of runners: Twenty-three
Winner: Ascetic's Silver (Mr. A. Hastings—10 st 9 lb)
Time: 9 minutes 34⅕ seconds

Ascetic's Silver, unofficially first the previous year, had been sold by his breeder, Mr. P. J. Dunne, to the German, Prince Hatzfeldt, and was ridden by his trainer, the Hon. Aubrey Hastings. The nine-year-old won by ten lengths without making a mistake, followed by Red Lad and Aunt May.

Among those to get round were Drumcree, Phil May, Wolf's Folly, Oatlands, Gladiator, and Ivor Anthony's mount, Crautacaun.

The year: 1907
Number of runners: Twenty-three
Winner: Eremon (A. Newey—10 st 1 lb)
Time: 9 minutes 47$\frac{1}{5}$ seconds

Ascetic's Silver was handicapped out of it at 12 st 7 lb, while Drumcree was thirteen years old. It was an undistinguished field, dominated from the start by Eremon, whose jockey, Alf Newey, lost an iron at the second fence and rode the rest of the race without it. To add to his troubles the riderless Rathvale harassed Eremon during the first circuit, jumping across and threatening to bring him down.

As they turned towards the country for the second time Rathvale finally swerved away, allowing Eremon to jump freely. Handicapped at only 10st 1 lb and receiving 34 lb from Ascetic's Silver, the seven-year-old increased his lead to fifty yards approaching Valentine's, where he frightened his supporters by jumping at an angle. But he made no mistake, coming away to win in a canter from Tom West and Patlander. Ravenscliffe was fourth, followed by Barabbas II, Ascetic's Silver, Buckaway II and Napper Tandy.

Eremon was trained by Tom Coulthwaite, who in 1931 was to delay his retirement in the hope of seeing Grakle win. Warned off in 1913 and not reinstated until 1930, he liked to boast that he had never ridden a horse in his life. Yet he had a genius for bringing out the best in long-distance stayers.

There's a story about Ravenscliffe. When he retired from racing he was sold by Mr. R. J. Hannam to a friend sixteen miles away. The old horse didn't approve the change. He jumped out of his field, cleared a railway gate and made good time to Mr. Hannam's window, where he nickered for a welcome.

The year: 1908
Number of runners: Twenty-four
Winner: Rubio (H. B. Bletsoe—10 st 5 lb)
Time: 10 minutes 3⅗ seconds

Other horses with American blood had become successful steeplechasers, but Rubio at ten years old was the first American-bred winner. He was born at the Rancho del Paso stud in California, where Mr. James Ben Ali Haggin regularly produced young horses for sale at Newmarket. Rubio was in the consignment of 1899. Nobody thought much of him and he was sold for only fifteen guineas to Major F. Douglas-Pennant, who turned him to grass with the intention of making him a hunter. Rubio proved better than that, winning three races as a five-year-old before breaking down.

Major Pennant then loaned him to the landlord of the Prospect Arms, Towcester, with the request that he be used to draw the horse bus from the hotel to the railway station and back again. There was a hope that regular trotting on the roads would restore his legs. The treatment worked. After three years of hammering from hotel to station, the eight-year-old was declared fit to race, although he seemed wrong in his wind.

W. Costello prepared him for Aintree, where he was ridden by H. B. Bletsoe, son of the owner of Grudon.

Despite his suspect legs and despite his wind, Rubio outstayed them all to win from Mattie MacGregor and The Lawyer III.

The year: 1909
Number of runners: Thirty-two
Winner: Lutteur III (G. Parfrement—10 st 11 lb)
Time: 9 minutes 53⅘ seconds

After the first success for an American breeder came the first all-French success; for although Huntsman had won for a French owner in 1862, he had been bred in Britain. Lutteur III was a five-year-old stallion, owned by Monsieur J. Hennessy, a member of the brandy family, and ridden by the French jockey, Georges Parfrement. He came to H. Escott's stable at Lewes for his final preparation, but his reputation was already established. Popular support made him joint favourite with Shady Girl in the biggest field since 1850.

Mattie MacGregor refused; Rubio fell; Shady Girl was baulked; that fine horse, Ascetic's Silver, broke down. In the last half-mile Lutteur III, jumping fluently and ridden with calm judgment by Parfrement, came from far back with a smooth run. Outsiders Judas and Caubeen chased him home, but after Rubio came down there was only one horse in it. For the first time since 1862 the cry '*Vive la France*' was heard at Aintree.

The decade ended with a sharp decline in the number of amateurs who rode regularly in steeplechases. For forty years the National Hunt Committee had struggled to sift the genuine from the bogus and to enforce professional status on those who rode for money. Slowly a new class of professional had emerged and one of the greatest was Arthur Nightingall, who won the National three times and had a second and four thirds in twelve other rides.

He was an accomplished exponent of the lean-back style of riding over fences. A contributor to *The Sportsman* wrote of him: 'I have often thought on seeing him landing over a fence with his horse's croup nearly touching his back, what a lot he must save his mount compared with the crouched-up images who are never off their horses' shoulders.'

Despite Nightingall's success, the 'free cant back' style was going out of favour and would soon be ridiculed.

10

King Edward VII died in 1910 and the Grand National lost a friend. King George V attended the National occasionally but did not share the love of racing, although his eldest son, when Prince of Wales, rode in point-to-points. Forty years would pass before another member of the Royal family gave steeplechasing patronage similar to that given by Edward VII.

The year: 1910
Number of runners: Twenty-five
Winner: Jenkinstown (R. Chadwick—10 st 5 lb)
Time: 10 minutes $4\frac{4}{5}$ seconds

A new name appeared in Aintree folk-lore; Jerry M, already winner of the Stanley, Becher and Valentine 'chases. The handicapper gave him 12 st 7 lb, 42 lb more than the bottom weights and 30 lb more than Jenkinstown, from the Coulthwaite stable at Hednesford which had sent Eremon to win in 1907. Jenkinstown had the same owner—Mr. S. Howard—and like Eremon, had been bought in Dublin from Mr. James Daly.

The race began with disasters at the first three fences, where more fell than throughout the rest of the race. Mr. F. Bibby had three runners, Caubeen, Glenside and Wickham. They all came down. At the end of the first circuit only ten were left of the original twenty-five.

Odor, ridden by his owner and neglected at 100—1, was among the leaders with Jerry M and Springbok. Then Springbok went, his saddle slipping. Shady Girl fell for the first time in thirty steeplechases. Algy Anthony, having his last National ride, broke two ribs when Judas came down. After Valentine's for the second time there were only two in it; Jenkinstown and Jerry M.

Jenkinstown kept going the better to give Mr. Howard his second win in four years with only his second entry. Odor was third, followed by Carsey and Fetlar's Pride.

The year: 1911
Number of runners: Twenty-six
Winner: Glenside (Mr. J. Anthony—10 st 5 lb)
Time: 10 minutes 4⅘ seconds

The newcomer was a rider; Jack Anthony, destined to become the greatest over Liverpool fences in his generation. He had the mount on Glenside, one of Mr. Bibby's three the previous year and considered unlucky to have been brought down.

The French were represented by Lutteur III, given 12 st 3 lb but backed to favouritism; and by M. de Mumm's six-year-old, Trianon III, carrying 11 st 8 lb. Jenkinstown was trying again and Caubeen and Rathnally were popular choices. But Jerry M was absent, having sustained an injury in France when winning the Paris Steeplechase.

It was less a race than a series of accidents which left only one horse on his feet and that a mediocrity, derided for his one eye and declared gone in the wind. As popular choices fell like heroes in a battle, Glenside was left galloping alone. The only excitement for the record crowd was whether he would run out of luck and reduce the race to the ultimate farce.

Anything might have happened, but Glenside that day had the help of an outstanding rider who got him through the muddle of fallen and loose horses, then kept him on his feet when he was looking for the end.

For the first time the winner finished alone. Rathnally was

remounted by Chadwick to finish second. Shady Girl, remounted by Clancy, finished third. The only other rider to get round was Mr. MacNeill, who caught his own horse, Foolhardy, and struggled up to win a private wager that he would complete the course.

The year: 1912
Number of runners: Twenty-four
Winner: Jerry M (E. Piggott—12st 7 lb)
Time: 10 minutes 13⅖ seconds

The prize was increased to £3,500 and Jerry M was back; already a 'character' to rival Manifesto and Cloister, as praised for his ability as Lottery had been, as admired as The Lamb for his amiable temperament. He was ridden by Ernie Piggott.

His owner was Mr. C. G. Duff, who had owned Cloister in 1893. Mr. Duff had inherited a baronetcy and had changed his name to Assheton-Smith. In 1908 he had come back to steeplechasing in the hope of finding another Cloister. Like many owners before and since, he had looked towards Ireland and heard about a horse, sired by Walmsgate and bred at Croom, in Co. Limerick, by Miss K. Hartigan. Mr. Widger, famous as a buyer of Aintree-type horses, had bought him as a yearling, calling him Jerry M in tribute to horse-breaker Jerry Mulclair.

Jerry M had won a few small races and was in the shop window at £800. Sir Edward Hulton had turned him down as thick in the wind; a defect which at first discouraged Assheton-Smith, who finally paid £1,200. Jerry M had won £6,000 in Paris, but during 1911 he'd proved difficult to train. Only the skill of trainer Bob Gore, born in Dublin with a stable at Findon, got him right for the race of 1912.

Jerry M had had only one preliminary race; at Hurst Park a few weeks before, when he'd beaten Bloodstone without trouble. Some doubted whether it could be enough, but Jerry M gave effective answer when he appeared in the paddock. He looked fit to run for his life and the public immediately made him 4—1 co-favourite with the Coulthwaite-trained Rathnally.

Among the lower weights was Covertcoat, while Jenkinstown had been sold to Mr. G. W. Blundell for £3,000. Lord Derby's Axle Pin was a popular place bet, for the Liverpool crowd trusted the local peer to give them a 'run for their money'.

Jenkinstown was lamed at the fence after Becher's and when the race for home began, Bloodstone, receiving 15 lb, seemed too fast for Jerry M. But Piggott's mount would not be beaten. By sheer stamina rather than superlative speed, the top weight kept with the challenger. At the last it was still a race, but the further they went the easier Jerry M made it appear. Poor Bloodstone, thoroughly discouraged, could get no nearer than six lengths with Axle Pin third.

The time of ten minutes thirteen seconds was twenty-four seconds slower than Manifesto in 1899 and thirty-one seconds slower than Cloister in 1893. But Jerry M was only the third to have carried 12 st 7 lb to victory. It was his greatest triumph and his last.

He damaged his pelvic muscles and had to rest. Long inactivity caused his wind to deteriorate and at ten years old he was declared a 'roarer'. Sir Charles Assheton-Smith retired him to North Wales and after the owner's death in 1914, Jerry M went back to trainer Gore at Findon. Not long afterwards he injured himself and had to be destroyed.

The year: 1913
Number of runners: Twenty-two
Winner: Covertcoat (P. Woodland—11 st 6 lb)
Time: 10 minutes 19 seconds

The story of the National is a story of luck; good luck and bad, mediocre horses winning and brilliant horses failing, rich owners spending fortunes without success, modest owners winning with horses who never won again. Sir Charles Assheton-Smith joined the lucky few when he bought two horses for about £2,000 and won with both.

Jerry M was one. The other was Covertcoat, bought at Dublin sales for 1,075 guineas; much inferior to his stable companion yet capable of winning if the luck was right. Sir Charles's luck was that the race became a shambles, highly fancied horses eliminating themselves before the chips were down. Percy Woodland's luck was already known. Ten years before he had picked up a chance ride on Drumcree and won. Now at the last moment he was available for Covertcoat.

Carsey was one of the luckless horses. Twice fourth and making his fifth appearance, he seemed to have the race won when he took a fatal liberty with the last. Covertcoat was left in front with Woodland looking over a shoulder for the rest.

Irish Mail was second, ridden by Owen Anthony. Carsey was remounted, jumped the last fence easily and finished a distant third.

The year: 1914
Number of runners: Twenty
Winner: Sunloch (W. J. Smith—9st 7 lb)
Time: 9 minutes 58⅘ seconds

Sir Charles Assheton-Smith almost pulled off the feat of winning three years in succession, for he tried to buy Sunloch about six months before the race. But the owner would not sell. Sunloch was a pet horse, trained and hunted by his owner, Mr. T. Tyler, then ridden in farmers' races. His jockey was the comparatively inexperienced W. J. Smith, who set out to make all the running and was at one stage forty lengths ahead.

More experienced jockeys sat quietly, waiting for him to 'come back'. C. Hawkins and A. Carter, on the French hopes Trianon III and Lutteur III, were among them, but Sunloch showed no signs of faltering as they approached Becher's for the second time.

Too late Hawkins and Carter realised that the owner-trained nonentity was running away from them. They sat down to ride and narrowed the gap, but by now the crowd was on the side of the run-away, cheering his every leap. There was a wail of dismay at the last, where Sunloch stumbled and was almost down. But he was up in an instant, like a boxer denying a knock-down, to sprint away from Trianon and Lutteur in a time only one second slower than Moifaa's in 1904.

Not since Count Kinsky and Zoedone had an owner become so identified with his horse. On his Loughborough farm Mr. Tyler had given countless hours to the preparation of the eight-year-old, and his jubilation in the paddock was vitally different from that shown in other years by professional owners who scarcely knew their horses.

The year: 1915
Number of runners: Twenty
Winner: Ally Sloper (Mr. J. Anthony—10 st 5 lb)
Time: 9 minutes 47⅘ seconds

Guns were blasting holes in a generation across the Channel and critics of the war effort were indignant that racing could continue on the slogan 'Business as usual'. Others considered sport to be as important to morale as theatres and music-halls. Uniforms lucky enough to be on leave on National day splashed patches of khaki and navy blue in the Aintree crowd as Ally Sloper won to make Lady Nelson the first woman to own the winner.

It was a perilous ride for Jack Anthony. He was nearly down at the second, saved only by his brother Ivor, who was alongside on Ilston. Ivor reached out and grabbed him and dragged him back. At the Canal ditch Ally Sloper blundered again and Jack was 'between his ears'. But on the second circuit the Hastings-trained six-year-old settled down, jumping sensibly and maintaining such a determined gallop that he was overtaking Jacobus at the last. He cleared it the better and ran away from Jacobus with Father Confessor third.

Until Lady Nelson's victory only three women had owned a National runner. They were Miss Norris, who became the owner of Wild Man From Borneo in 1897, two years after his success; Mrs. Widger, the owner of Sunny Shower in 1901; and Lady Torrington who owned Circassian's Pride in 1911. But none had ever looked like winning until Lady Nelson paid £700

The first fence in 1951. Eleven horses came down, reducing the race to a shambles. Nickel Coin (J. Bullock) stood up to win

Big cheers for the winner Sheila's Cottage (Arthur Thompson) after winning in 1948

Incredible scenes at Aintree as Tipperary Tim (Mr. W. P. Dutton) is led in after winning in 1928

Over the first in 1958, with the favourite Wyndburgh (6) keeping out of trouble towards the right

Jumping Becher's on the first circuit in 1968. Seventeen of the forty-five got round

The start in 1929, when a record number of sixty-six ran. Gregalach won at 100—1

Sundew (F. Winter) comes down at Becher's in 1956. Devon Loch (R. Francis) and E.S.B. (D. V. Dick) went on to a memorable climax, Devon Loch collapsing with the race apparently won for a brown horse by Travelling Lad, bred in Lincolnshire by Mr. C. Hill and sold at Doncaster for twenty-five guineas to Mr. S. E. Armitage. One-time jockey H. Randall saw possibilities in the horse and bought him from Mr. Armitage, then resold him to Lady Nelson. The victory was in key with the campaign for equality for women.

At the end of 1915 Aintree was taken over by the War Office and closed to racing. The National was transferred to Gatwick and called 'The Racecourse Association Steeplechase', with the prize reduced to £500. Vermouth won at 100—8, followed by Irish Mail, Schoolmoney and Jacobus. Ally Sloper was eighth in a field of twenty-one.

In 1917 the name was changed to 'The War National Steeplechase'. It was won by Ballymacad, trained by Hastings and ridden by Driscoll; although Limerock must have won if he had not collapsed a few yards from the post. Chang was second, Ally Sloper third and Vermouth fourth.

The last substitute National in 1918 was the best of the three. Poethlyn won for Mrs. H. Peel from Captain Dreyfus and Ballymacad. Ally Sloper and Vermouth tried again while Sergeant Murphy and Shaun Spadah appeared for the first time.

The year: 1919
Number of runners: Twenty-two
Winner: Poethlyn (E. Piggott—12 st 7 lb.)
Time: 10 minutes 8⅖ seconds

The war was over. 'Victory' had not yet become a sour joke and 'a land fit for heroes' was still the politicians' promise. Men celebrated their release from trench, destroyer and merchant ship by rushing to Aintree for a race which seemed to stand for England in a shattered world. Crowds were larger than ever before; the mood was a desperate gaiety. It was a day when the favourite had to win and Poethlyn, after his success at Gatwick, was a hot favourite at 11—4.

The field included past winners Sunloch, Vermouth and Ally Sloper, and future winners Sergeant Murphy and Shaun

Spadah. Eleven got round but nothing could stay with the favourite after Valentine's for the second time. In some hands Poethlyn could be a random jumper, but Ernie Piggott 'knew him backwards' and got him round an easy winner from Ballyboggan and Pollen. The Irish horse, Ballyboggan, was ridden by Willie Head, the father of Alec who trained Lavandin to win the Derby of 1956.

Poethlyn joined the élite who had won in successive years and shared with Cloister, Jerry M and Manifesto the distinction of winning with 12 st 7 lb. Mrs. Peel became the first woman to own the winner in successive years. In what might be called an Aintree tradition, Poethlyn had begun humbly, sold for £7 to a hotelier in Shrewsbury, then bought by Mr. Peel for fifty guineas and given to his wife.

11

Grand Nationals of the 1920s were run against a back-cloth of internal strife; on the one hand those who wished to retain a way of life which the war had interrupted, on the other those who were determined to introduce social and political changes. The voices of mill-worker and miner were being heard and the patriotic hysteria which had celebrated victory in Europe had quickly soured to conflict between the widely separated strata of British society. To the Manchester cotton-worker the enemy was the aristocrat; to the aristocrat the enemy was the 'mob'. Yet they came together at Aintree on National day, prejudices and fears forgotten as they watched the greatest race of the year produce its heroes.

The first hero of the 1920s was among the greatest of all time; described by his rider as a 'steam engine' and accorded a guard of honour by celebrating Irishmen. That horse was Troytown, still talked about in the back-street pubs of Merseyside when old races are relived across the dark pints.

The year: 1920
Number of runners: Twenty-four
Winner: Troytown (Mr. J. Anthony—11 st 9 lb)
Time: 10 minutes 20⅕ seconds

King George V was there in a howling gale to see the mighty

Troytown, declared by Jack Anthony to be the most difficult ride in his experience, power down first-class opposition to win 'like a hurricane'. At the end Anthony's arms were numb. Ruefully he admitted himself much more tired than Troytown seemed to be.

Poethlyn was favourite, despite top weight. Troytown was 6—1. The field included Ballyboggan, Turkey Buzzard, Loch Allen, All White and Picture Saint. Mr. H. Brown, riding his self-trained The Bore, represented the genuine amateur in a sport now dominated by professionals.

Poethlyn fell at the first and Troytown led them into the rain-haze on the far side. For more than a mile little could be seen from the stands. When the first shape emerged, it was identified as Troytown, pulling Anthony's arms out. The rest were toiling and the Irish were already cheering as Troytown jumped the water ten lengths clear.

He was seen to make only one mistake and that four fences out. He slipped as he prepared to take off and crashed through the top, tearing a gap like shell-fire. A lesser horse must have fallen, but Troytown was not only big and brave. He had the dexterity which marks a great steeplechaser. By some miracle he found an 'extra leg' and kept himself off the floor.

For a moment it seemed that Mr. Brown's The Bore might get the better of him, but Troytown recovered his stride and was only a length behind The Bore as they jumped the next. It was an incredible jump, for Troytown touched down a length in front and thundered joyfully towards the first of the fences on the racecourse. His ears were pricked, listening to the cheers. He jumped the last as eagerly as he had jumped the first, having so much in hand at the finish that Anthony could scarcely convince him it was over.

The Turk II squeezed The Bore out of second place. Sergeant Murphy and Neurotic were others to finish.

Troytown was bred by his owner, Major Thomas Gerrard of Co. Meath. He was not raced until he was six and much of his strength and zest could be attributed to this slow development. He won the Paris Steeplechase and the Champion 'Chase in 1919 and was in his prime at Aintree in 1920.

The manner of his victory suggested he might become another Manifesto, but his career was ended before he could face the supreme test of carrying 12 st 7 lb. He returned to France for the Paris race and finished third; a better performance than it seemed, for he was delayed en route by a dock strike. Five days later he ran in the Prix des Drags over two miles six furlongs, but made a mistake at a brook fence and broke his leg above the knee. Even then he was not finished. He dragged himself up and tried to continue, finally collapsing in a way that broke the heart of the French crowd. He was destroyed at once and buried at Asnières, where a headstone marks the grave.

Jack Anthony, son of a Carmarthenshire farmer, began in point-to-points and rode his first winner under National Hunt rules at Ludlow in 1906 when he was sixteen. He won three Nationals as an amateur on Glenside, Ally Sloper and Troytown, then turned professional in 1920. When he retired from riding in 1927, he began training at Letcombe Regis and prepared Easter Hero for the sensational race of 1928.

The year: 1921
Number of runners: Thirty-five
Winner: Shaun Spadah (*F. Rees—11 st 7 lb*)
Time: 10 minutes 26 seconds

King George and Queen Mary, with the Prince of Wales, Princess Mary and Prince Henry, watched a record field go to the start. There was such chaos in the early stages that after the first circuit only All White, Turkey Buzzard, Shaun Spadah, The Bore and Glencorrig were left.

Shaun Spadah nearly came down at the water and Glencorrig refused at 'Fan's Fence'. All White was frightened by newspapers blown by the wind. He shied as he jumped and although he got over, he dropped Chadwick in the process. The jockey held on and struggled back to the saddle, but his chance was lost.

Bonnie Charlie fell four times. American-born Morgan Blair kept remounting, determined to win a private bet that he would get round. Shaun Spadah and The Bore had the race to themselves until The Bore fell at the last. His owner Harry Brown broke a collar-bone yet heaved himself back and continued to ride with his left hand. The Bore finished second with All White third.

Shaun Spadah, the only horse to remain on his feet throughout, was bred in Co. Meath by Mr. P. McKenna and sold to Mr. R. Cleary, who sent him to Algy Anthony at the Curragh for one race on the flat. After that he drifted from owner to owner until Mr. M. H. Benson passed him on to Mr. (later Sir) T. M. McAlpine, whose trainer was George Poole at Lewes.

George had ridden his first winner over fences at thirteen and had a way with jumpers. Under his guidance Shaun Spadah developed as a steeplechaser and his greatest triumph was hailed as an all-British success; for Shaun Spadah was Irish-bred, Scottish-owned, English-trained and ridden by F. Rees, son of a Welsh veterinary surgeon.

The year: 1922
Number of runners: Thirty-two
Winner: Music Hall (L. B. Rees—11 st 8 lb)
Time: 9 minutes $55\frac{4}{5}$ seconds

Music Hall was bred by Mrs. F. Blacker in Co. Kildare, then sold to Mrs. M. Stokes of Market Harborough. She won the Scottish National with him in 1920 before selling him to Mr. H. Kershaw. A good horse with 'groggy' legs, he was one of the first to be trained by Owen Anthony, brother of Jack.

It says much for Owen Anthony's skill and care that Music Hall came to Aintree apparently restored and confidently backed at 100—9. He was ridden by L. B. Rees, brother of the winning jockey in 1921 and father of Billy Rees.

The favourite, Southampton, came down at the first with Harry Brown, who had ridden The Bore with one hand the previous year. Shaun Spadah fell at the same time; Sergeant Murphy slipped into the Canal ditch when leading; All White, Norton and General Saxham came down in a heap; Awbeg broke his neck at Becher's; Clashing Arms slipped up; Arravale toppled over Becher's on the second circuit, falling on the dead Awbeg.

Out of the confusion three were still going strongly; Music Hall, Double Escape and Drifter. Double Escape fell, to be chased and remounted by Captain Bennet. Drifter cut a coronet so badly that part of the foot was hanging, yet he continued from Valentine's on three legs. He almost fell at the last, then struggled home twelve lengths behind Music Hall. Taffytus, ridden by nineteen-year-old Ted Leader, was third, followed by Sergeant Murphy who had lost his bridle.

There was a sad sequel for Music Hall. Having run at Manchester and finished second, he crossed the Channel for the Paris Steeplechase in June. He was in front with his field well beaten when his patched-up legs finally collapsed.

The year: 1923
Number of runners: Twenty-seven
Winner: Sergeant Murphy (*Captain G. H. Bennet—11 st 3 lb*)
Time: 9 minutes 36 seconds

Since the success of American-bred Rubio in 1908, Americans had taken an increasing interest in the National; much more, in fact, than they would ever take in the Derby or St. Leger. The first American owner to win was Mr. Stephen Sandford, an undergraduate at Cambridge University whose father had given him Sergeant Murphy as a hunter. 'The Sergeant' proved a handful, so Stephen returned him to training with George Blackwell and it was in the Sandford colours that Sergeant Murphy had finished fourth to Music Hall.

He came back to Aintree at the age of thirteen for his luckiest race. His rider was the persistent Captain Bennet, nicknamed 'Tuppy', who had made getting round the next best thing to winning. With 11 st 3 lb Sergeant Murphy was receiving 18 lb from another veteran, Shaun Spadah, and American support backed him down to 100—6. More favoured were Forewarned, Arravale, Libretto and Taffytus.

Forewarned, Libretto and Taffytus fell on the first circuit. Masterful was killed. Drifter led at the water from Sergeant Murphy and Shaun Spadah. Arravale was well placed at Becher's on the second circuit, where he jumped awkwardly as though remembering his fright of the previous year when he had come down on a dead horse. Conjuror II, harassed by a loose horse and suffering grievously from a cut tongue, was prominent three out, followed by Shaun Spadah, Drifter, Punt Gun and Sergeant Murphy.

Twelve-year-old Shaun Spadah ran gallantly under 12 st 7 lb but was 'out on his feet' approaching the last. He could not catch Sergeant Murphy, the first thirteen-year-old to win since Why Not in 1894. Conjuror II was six lengths away third. Drifter finished again, accompanied by Max, Punt Gun, and the grey without a pedigree, Cinders II.

Sergeant Murphy's long career still was not done. He continued racing until he was sixteen, when he fell at Bogside and broke a leg.

The year: 1924
Number of runners: Thirty-one
Winner: Master Robert (R. Trudgill—10 st 5 lb)
Time: 9 minutes 40 seconds

This was the year of the 'plough-horse', jointly owned by Lord Airlie and Major S. Green and ridden by Bob Trudgill, whose previous National record was four rides, four falls, all on bad horses.

Master Robert, bred by Mr. R. McKinley, was judged too slow for racing and at the age of five came back to the farm. Mr. McKinley kept him busy in the plough, and the huge horse raised no serious objections. But the farmer had 'too many horses' and sold Master Robert for £50. Finally he passed into the ownership of Lord Airlie and Sidney Green. They sent him to Wroughton to be trained by Aubrey Hastings, whose previous winners were Ascetic's Silver, Ballymacad and Ally Sloper.

The ex-plough horse was found to have a diseased bone in his foot. Only constant poulticing could relieve him of pain and he became the special charge of Frank Cundell, the Swindon veterinary surgeon. Steady work on the roads helped to restore the foot, but he was never wholly sound and pulled up lame after running at Wolverhampton only a week before Liverpool.

Mr. Peter Roberts refused the ride and it was offered to Bob Trudgill, a brave jump-jockey who had taken as many falls as most and was to take another on Charlie Wise the day before the National. Jack Moloney was asked to stand by, but Trudgill wasn't the kind to give in, however slim the hope of success. He weighed out for what was to be the race of his life.

Conjuror II, a defiant third the previous year, was 5—2 favourite. Others well backed were Taffytus, Fly Mask, Silvo, Shaun Spadah and Sergeant Murphy, while All White, Drifter, Arravale, Double Escape and Libretto were trying again. Palm Oil was ridden by Peter Roberts, who had rejected Master Robert.

Conjuror fell at Becher's; Sergeant Murphy blundered at the water; Arravale refused at Becher's on the second circuit in exactly the fashion of the previous year; Old Tay Bridge fell with Hubert Hartigan when going well. At that stage Silvo, bought by Mr. W. H. Midwood for 10,500 guineas, seemed the probable winner, but Master Robert would not be shaken off.

Silvo, destined to win big races but never the National, capitulated before the last, where Fly Mask put in a strong challenge. But Trudgill was riding like the inspired and his ex-plough horse responded to win by four lengths, with Silvo three lengths third.

Shaun Spadah, making his last appearance at the age of thirteen, got round. So did Drifter, Sergeant Murphy, and Wavetown. But Palm Oil came down with the luckless Roberts.

Trudgill collapsed as he slid from his horse, scarcely able

to stagger to the weighing-in scales with saddle and weight-cloth. Another jockey, Arthur Stubbs, who had ridden Chin Chin, gave him the highest praise: 'No other jockey but Trudgill could have won on Master Robert.'

The year: 1925
Number of runners: Thirty-three
Winner: Double Chance (Major J. P. Wilson—10 st 9 lb)
Time: 9 minutes 42⅖ seconds

After the plough horse with the injured foot came the gift horse Double Chance, bred at Southcourt by Mr. Anthony de Rothschild, trained at Palace House by John Watson, found to be unsound and given by Mr. Rothschild to Fred Archer, grandson of William Archer who had ridden Little Charlie in 1858.

Archer had served under Mr. Rothschild in the Royal Bucks Hussars and had set up as a trainer at Malton. He hunted Double Chance for a time, got him sound enough to win at Wetherby, then fired him severely and won five small races before selling a share to Liverpool cotton-broker, Mr. D. Goold. Double Chance had never seen an Aintree fence when Major Wilson, a war pilot who had shot down a Zeppelin over Hull, rode him towards the new starting gate.

Old Tay Bridge was favourite, with Silvo and Fly Mask among the popular choices. Drifter had been bought by Mr. Sandford, who had won with Sergeant Murphy. He led on the first circuit, then dropped back as Double Chance, Silvo and Old Tay Bridge took over. Sprig, Jack Horner and Max were also prominent, but when Silvo faded, Fly Mask ridden by Major E. C. Doyle with what seemed to be a 'double handfull', was left in front with Old Tay Bridge.

As they approached the last, Fly Mask seemed a probable winner, but Double Chance was coming strongly to win by four lengths from Old Tay Bridge. Fly Mask was a disappointing third.

Sprig was fourth and Silvo, carrying 12 st 7 lb, fifth. Jack Horner was ridden by Morgan Blair. The American had again backed himself to get round and again he won his bet.

The year: 1926
Number of runners: Thirty
Winner: Jack Horner (W. Watkinson—10 st 5 lb)
Time: 9 minutes 36 seconds

It was the year when social conflict exploded in the general strike. Crowds came to Aintree to escape the front-page news. Americans were there in hundreds, their enthusiasm whetted by Mr. Sandford's success in 1923 and by the exploits of Morgan Blair.

Mr. Sandford was represented by Bright's Boy and Mount Etna, but another American horse, Ballinode, owned by Colonel Alger of Detroit, was found to be wrong shortly before the race and had to be withdrawn. George Blackwell, on behalf of Colonel Alger, tried unsuccessfully to buy another.

Mr. A. C. Schwartz was luckier. An American polo player, he arrived from New York a month before the race, bought Jack Horner from Mr. K. Mackay for 4,000 guineas and within a fortnight got his money back.

Silvo, Sprig and Old Tay Bridge were among the favourites, while there was plenty of support for Koka and Mount Etna. Jack Horner and Bright's Boy were 25—1. Silvo fell at the first, but scrambled up to lead the rest on the first circuit. Lone Hand was killed. Darracq, ridden by F. Gurney, led them into the country for the second time, with Jack Horner among the leading group. Sprig and Old Tay Bridge were prominent.

Excited Americans kept their glasses focused on Bright's Boy as they came away from Valentine's. Mr. Sandford's second choice, believed inferior to Mount Etna, was still in front at the last, but Jack Horner took over on the flat, holding off Old Tay Bridge by three lengths. Bright's Boy was a tired third, followed by Sprig and Darracq.

Jack Horner had once been sold in a draft of hunters for 125 guineas. Trained by H. Leader, he was never better than at

Aintree on this day. Shortly afterwards he broke down and was retired. His little-known jockey, forty-year-old Watkinson, Tasmanian-born, was killed three weeks later in a steeplechase at Bogside.

The year: 1927
Number of runners: Thirty-seven
Winner: Sprig (T. Leader—12 st 4 lb)
Time: 10 minutes 10$\frac{1}{5}$ seconds

The gradual increase in the number of runners could be regarded as a compliment to the popularity of steeplechasing and owed something to the participation of American owners. It was also considered a comment on the terms of qualification.

The National had never lacked critics and the critics now were adamant that the conditions of the race needed to be tightened in the hope of excluding mediocre horses and reducing the risks of pile-up. No changes were to be made for several years, but one innovation of great importance was the nation-wide commentary broadcast by the B.B.C. The first commentators were Meyrick Good and George Allison.

Sprig was 8—1; All White was trying again at thirteen and his owner, Lord Wavertree, would always consider him unlucky; but remarkably the field included no previous winner. Among the new horses was the five-year-old Grakle, giving Jack Moloney his first ride in a National.

Thrown In, ridden by the Hon. Hugh Grosvenor, son of Lord Stalbridge, fell at the first. Grecian Wave ran out when in the lead and Grakle faltered at the Canal ditch. On the second circuit Sprig took over, putting in such a leap at Becher's that he cleared two fallen horses and brought back memories of Troytown.

Sprig cut his off-fore but gave no sign of lameness as he galloped towards the Canal fence. There he put in one of the most remarkable jumps ever seen at Aintree. Taking off fifth, he passed three horses in the air and landed with the pace-maker. Bright's Boy went with him and they seemed to have the race to themselves until Bovril III, a one-eyed outsider, ridden by the inexperienced amateur, Mr. Gerald Pennington, put in such a challenge that Ted Leader on Sprig and Jack Anthony on Bright's Boy were soon riding for their lives.

Sprig won by a length from Bovril III, with Bright's Boy third and Drinmond, owned by Lord Queenborough, fourth. The winner was owned by seventy-four-year-old Mrs. M. Partridge, who loved the horse because he'd been bred in 1917 by her son. The son was killed in 1918, shortly before the Armistice, but in his letters home he'd always planned to race the horse. His mother fulfilled that intent, sending Sprig to Tom Leader at Newmarket, where he showed considerable ability over hurdles and fences. To win the National was the ultimate ambition and the Leader family shared the widowed mother's determination. That was why Ted Leader, son of the trainer, refused rides on other horses, including an offer of £2,000.

The year: 1928
Number of runners: Forty-two
Winner: Tipperary Tim (Mr. W. P. Dutton—10 st)
Time: 10 minutes 23⅖ seconds

The record field was condemned dangerous. There were alarms that in the cavalry charge for the first fence, one faller would bring down others to the peril of perhaps a dozen jockeys. Yet the threat bred caution and when they came away from the first, not one horse or jockey was down. The stands sighed with relief, but relief was premature. Disasters were to come so that for the second time in the history of the race, only one horse was to get round without mishap.

Easter Hero, sold by Mr. Barbour to Mr. A. Lowenstein for £7,000, led them towards Becher's and jumped it with spectacular ease. He looked what he was declared to be; the best horse in the race, perhaps in the country. As he approached the Canal ditch he gave no hint of what was to come. He seemed to swerve, to think about refusal. Some witnesses swore that he slipped. But the sequence of events was so swift that those gathered near the fence could not be sure what or why or when.

Easter Hero crashed on top of the fence and straddled it, apparently stuck, baulking those behind and putting more than twenty out of the race. Not until Popham Down in 1967 was there to be a mêlée like it.

Only nine were still there at the end of the first circuit. The French mare Maguelonne, ridden by Bedeloup, was prominent. So was the American, Billy Barton, trained by Aubrey Hastings and ridden by Tommy Cullinan. This grandson of Ardpatrick had won big races on the flat in Virginia before proving himself over timber.

Two from home there were only three left. Among them was Great Span, trained by Bill Payne and ridden by his seventeen-year-old son. He looked to be going the best after Maguelonne fell at Valentine's, but his saddle slipped, dumping young Payne and leaving Billy Barton clear.

The Americans began to cheer as Billy Barton approached the last, accompanied by the riderless Great Span. The only challenger was Tipperary Tim and few had noticed him in the parade or could even find his name on the race-card. Billy Barton must have won if he'd stood up. But he came down at the last, worried perhaps by Great Span. The fates were kinder to the tubed outsider, Tipperary Tim. He escaped interference and got over, then kept plodding to win the first race of his life. Cullinan remounted Billy Barton to finish second, but no horse was placed third.

Bred by Mr. J. Ryan, a rugby international, Tipperary Tim was sold as a yearling for £50 and at ten years old was owned by Mr. H. Kenyon and trained by J. Dodd. He came to Aintree with the reputation of being a 'thoroughly bad horse'. His success at 100—1 proved that truly 'anything could happen' and did more than any other thing to encourage owners to enter any horse, however mediocre, in the hope that luck would shine.

The year: 1929
Number of runners: Sixty-six
Winner: Gregalach (R. Everett—11 st 4 lb)
Time: 9 minutes 47⅖ seconds

The Aintree executive tried to stem the flood of entries by increasing the cost of starting to £100 and by introducing two additional stages at which horses could be withdrawn. But the prize of £5,000, plus the value of the sweepstake, was too high for owners to resist. Even to finish fourth was equal to winning a minor race elsewhere; for the fourth received £150, while the prizes to second and third were as high as £700 and £400.

The Canal ditch was filled; a change which helped to make Easter Hero, ridden by Jack Moloney, an overwhelming favourite despite his weight of 12 st 7 lb. He had won the Cheltenham Gold Cup impressively and there were many who thought him capable of becoming the first to achieve the double.

Great Span was second favourite at 100—6, with the American hero, Billy Barton, at 20—1. But American loyalties were divided, for Easter Hero had been bought by Mr. J. H. Whitney, later to become United States Ambassador to Britain. Never had the American 'hand' seemed so strong. For weeks cross-Atlantic liners had been packed with Americans determined to see the race.

Fortunately the starter got the massive field away quickly and Easter Hero went to the front at once. Again the first fence presented hazards and again they all got over safely. Easter Hero led them over Becher's, but as they approached the Canal fence, scene of débâcle the previous year, Moloney allowed others to give him a lead. Easter Hero seemed not to remember or to care. He jumped it with ridiculous ease and throughout the rest of the circuit he was strolling in front, ears pricked, aware of the applause as he jumped the water.

Only nineteen were still following. Sprig, Bright's Boy, Great Span and Tipperary Tim had fallen. On the second circuit it was still Easter Hero, so outclassing the rest that only cruel luck could stop him. There was a moment of alarm as he returned to the Canal. Moloney again eased him, allowing Richmond II and Shady Hook to come alongside. But Easter Hero dismissed alarms with another derisive jump and made the next seem a hurdle. Then Moloney felt his stride shorten.

The potential champion was suddenly in trouble, unable to shake off Gregalach. At the last they were still fighting it out, but slowly the 100—1 outsider, receiving 17 lb and boldly ridden by Everett, drew away to win by six lengths. Richmond II was third and nine got round, including Mellerays Belle and Grakle.

The cause of Easter Hero's collapse was soon explained. He had spread a plate with about half a mile remaining, twisting it to the shape of a letter 'S'. A sharp edge had gashed the ankle-boot on the other foreleg. Only a gallant horse could have got so near and it says much for Moloney's judgment that even when he saw victory slipping away, he did not use the whip. Afterwards he said, 'I wouldn't take a whip to the Hero. If he slowed down you knew he had given all he had.'

Gregalach, the second 100—1 outsider to win in successive years, was much superior to Tipperary Tim and was never again so under-rated. His owner, Mrs. M. A. Gemmell, had paid £5,000 for him as a five-year-old and her prize of £13,000 was four times greater than Mrs. Peel had received in 1919 when Poethlyn won. It was a second success for Tom Leader and a first for former Naval officer, Bob Everett, who became the first Australian-born jockey to win.

12

Radio was bringing the National home to those who had never seen Aintree, who might not even care about any other race of the year. The first commentary in 1927 had reached comparatively few, for receivers cost money and the service was slow in developing to small towns and villages where National Hunt racing was the principal sport. But from the first there had been one or two receivers in each working-class street, and the custom was for windows and doors to be opened so that others could hear while the privileged leaned towards the unseen voice, their faces intent, glaring at whoever dared to interrupt.

By the 1930s 'the wireless' had become part of the furniture in the homes of miner, mill-worker and farm-hand. Models were big and upright. They no longer needed long aerials. Reception was good in most parts of Britain, although in some corners families and neighbours sat around in a fury of frustration as the crackle of 'atmospherics' shattered the commentary. There was nothing more infurating than to own a wireless yet not to know what had won the National the instant it was won.

The B.B.C. took major sporting events seriously and its broadcast of the National, omitting only mention of betting, was from the first a technical feat implemented by increasingly professional production.

At the same time news-reel cameras recorded parts of the race and the films filtered down from West End palaces to remote 'flea-pits' where faces sat on benches and 'saw it happening' three weeks late.

Popular newspapers, aware of the rise in interest, especially among women who formed a high proportion of the radio audience, prepared simplified maps of the course and provided details about horses, jockeys and owners. Women were encouraged to have 'sixpence each way'. It was probably their only bet of the year and they had it without real hope of winning. Their need was to participate, if only from a distance. William Lynn would have been delighted.

The year: 1930
Number of runners: Forty-one
Winner: Shaun Goilin (T. Cullinan—11 st 7 lb)
Time: 9 minutes 40⅗ seconds

The runners were twenty-five fewer than the previous year, yet eleven more than in 1920. Gregalach, the 100—1 surprise of 1929, was among the favourites. So was his stable companion Grakle, thought by Tom Coulthwaite to be the better of the two. Mr. Whitney's colours were carried by Sir Lindsay in the absence through injury of Easter Hero.

There was also Shaun Goilin, sired by an unbroken colt in a field at Tipperary and sold as a yearling for twenty-two guineas. He had finally reached the ownership of Mr. W. H. Midwood, who had paid high for Silvo in the hope of winning a National. Trained by Frank Hartigan, the nephew of Garrett Moore who had won on The Liberator in 1879, Shaun Goilin was to take part in the greatest finish since 1882, when Lord Manners on Seaman shocked Tommy Beasley on Cyrus to strike a blow for the amateur against tough professionalism.

Old favourites Billy Barton, Bright's Boy, Tipperary Tim, Sprig and Darracq had gone with the 1920s. The new American hope was the grey hunter, Glangesia, sent from Pennsylvania by Mr. Bruce in the hope of succeeding where Billy Barton and

Easter Hero had failed. He shared the early lead with Gate Book, another grey, then went on his own to raise American hopes. At Valentine's for the second time he was overhauled by the eleven-year-old mare Mellerays Belle, fourth the previous year.

Two fences out she was joined by Shaun Goilin, running the race of his life, and by Sir Lindsay, the mount of Dudley Williams. They came to the last in line. Sir Lindsay stumbled and Williams lost both irons. Shaun Goilin and Mellerays Belle also made mistakes, each jockey continuing with a stirrup empty. Briefly Mason had the mare in front, but Shaun Goilin, strongly ridden by Tommy Cullinan who would have ridden Easter Hero, fought back to win by a neck.

Sir Lindsay, sired by Roi Herode who was the sire of The Tetrarch, came off worst in the mix-up at the last. He made a lot of ground to finish third, only a length and a half away. From the stands it seemed that he was an unlucky loser. There was plenty of sympathy for his owner, Mr. Whitney, who had had his share of bad luck with Easter Hero the previous year.

The year: 1931
Number of runners: Forty-three
Winner: Grakle (R. B. Lyall—11 st 7 lb)
Time: 9 minutes 32⅕ seconds

Easter Hero was back again, the winner of six races since 1929, including two Gold Cups. Ridden by F. Rees, he was favourite at 5—1 with Mellerays Belle 8—1 and Grakle 100—6. Czechoslovakia was represented by Gyi Lovam, ridden by Captain Popler. The American challenger was again Glangesia.

In summer weather the pace was fast from the start. Thirty were still standing at the end of the first circuit. Gregalach, jumping stylishly, led them into the country, followed by Easter Hero and Grakle. Drin broke his hock. Swift Rowland, falling at Becher's, was killed by another horse. Solanum blundered into Easter Hero, and the luckless favourite, destined to be the best horse never to win a National, came down with Theras. When he struggled up, he caused more trouble. His reins flopped over Ballasport's stirrup, dragging the leather from the saddle and almost taking jockey Williams' foot with it. With great courage Williams continued to ride a strong challenge as Kilbuck and Georginatown followed Gregalach and Grakle towards the last.

Grakle jumped it about a length clear of Gregalach, but Ballasport came down in a mix-up with Georginatown and Kilbuck. For more than 400 yards it was a straight fight between former stable companions. Their names had been linked in partnership for years. Both had been owned by Mr. T. K. Laidlaw and put up for sale simultaneously; both had been trained by Tom Coulthwaite, who had won with Eremon in 1907 and Jenkinstown in 1910, and both had won their reputations the hard way.

Many thought Gregalach the superior and a hundred yards out he seemed to be proving it. Carrying 12 st and giving Grakle 7 lb, he got his head in front but Jack Moloney could not keep it there. The final yards were too much for him and when his head bobbed in acknowledgment of defeat, Grakle drew away with every stride to win by one and a half lengths.

The veteran Coulthwaite, neither idle nor silent during his years 'in the wilderness', had always declared Grakle to be the superior and had delayed his retirement in expectation of Grakle's success. The son of Jackdaw seemed to realise what was expected of him. Not only did he win at the fifth attempt, but he lowered by two seconds the record set by Ascetic's Silver in 1906.

Annandale, 100—1, was third, followed by the French horse, Rhyticere, Shaun Goilin, Glangesia, Mellerays Belle, Great Span, Starbox, Harewood and Royal Arch II.

The luckiest man in England wasn't owner Mr. C. R. Taylor, who had paid £4,000 for Grakle and had waited five years for victory. The luckiest was Mr. Emilio Scala, of Battersea Park

Road, London, who held the winning ticket in the first 'Irish Sweep'. The prize was £354,544 but Mr. Scala had sold a half-share to Mr. Bendir, chief of the bookmaking firm of Ladbroke.

Total subscriptions were £1,755,963, of which £1,181,815 was distributed in prizes. They were astronomical figures in a sport which since 1837 had lived on crumbs and which as recently as 1929 had considered £13,000 a fantastic sum.

The year: 1932
Number of runners: Thirty-six
Winner: Forbra (J. Hamey—10 st 7 lb)
Time: 9 minutes 44⅗ seconds

The conditions were at last altered. Qualification was confined to horses who 'at the time of entry' had been placed in a steeplechase of not less than three miles and worth at least £200 to the winner, or in a steeplechase of any distance at Aintree.

The critics were not satisfied. Mediocre horses could still qualify because steeplechases of three miles on park courses were often contested by small fields; especially in bad weather or in the early months of the season. A horse had only to finish 'last of three' to be on his way to Aintree. Moreover the qualification need not be recent. A horse who finished 'last of three' at the age of five was still considered eligible for the National eight years later.

Grakle was back for the sixth and last time, carrying 12 st 3 lb and ridden by Jack Fawcus. He shared favouritism with Heartbreak Hill, an Irish mare owned by Mrs. C. S. Bird. Gregalach was there, too, ridden by leading amateur, Mr. F. R. Thackeray. But Easter Hero had passed from the scene of near-triumph to America, where owner Mr. Whitney showed him to admirers at hunt meets.

A newcomer was Forbra, declared to be 'the horse which couldn't fall'; schooled by T. F. Rimell at Kinnersley, ridden by the Cheltenham jockey Hamey and owned by Mr. W. Parsonage, of Ludlow, who had bought him for 1,500 guineas from Mrs. Hunt, of Rutland.

It was heartbreak day for supporters of Heartbreak Hill. The mare was going fluently when baulked by the riderless Pelorous Jack. O'Grady pulled her out of a wing and took her back for another attempt, but she had lost too much ground to challenge again. Grakle was baulked; Gregalach fell so heavily that amateur Thackeray was unconscious for a fortnight and never rode in a race again; K.C.B. was killed. Annandale came down at the last when chasing Forbra and Egremont.

These two, both on 10 st 7 lb, had jumped about ten fences in unison. They came to the last together with only inches between them. Forbra, a flat race reject with speed in his breeding, landed first on the flat and pulled away to win by three lengths. Egremont was ridden by Mr. E. Paget, a London stockbroker.

Shaun Goilin carried his 12 st 4 lb into third place. Others to finish were Near East, Aspirant, Heartbreak Hill, the remounted Annandale and far back, Sea Soldier.

The year: 1933
Number of runners: Thirty-four
Winner: Kellsboro' Jack (D. Williams—11 st 9 lb)
Time: 9 minutes 28 seconds

The quality of top-class steeplechasers was demonstrated by consistently fast times. Since 1922 only two winners—Sprig and Tipperary Tim—had been outside ten minutes. Kellsboro' Jack's time was a new record, four seconds faster than Grakle in 1931 and six seconds faster than Ascetic's Silver in 1906.

Kellsboro' Jack was named after his birthplace in Co. Meath. Mr. Ambrose Clark bought him as a yearling and sold him to Mrs. Clark for £1 at the joking suggestion of trainer Ivor Anthony. It was in her colours that the seven-year-old came to Aintree for one of the most spectacular races ever seen.

Golden Miller was there for the first time. He had already won the Cheltenham Gold Cup twice, but experts doubted that he was robust enough for Aintree. The public had no such doubts. They backed him joyfully to make him 9—1 favourite, despite his inexperience of Aintree and his massive weight of 12 st 2 lb.

Forbra and Heartbreak Hill were trying again. Southern Hero was a popular choice. The seventeen hands Remus, trained by Frank Morgan on a diet which included stout, became entangled in the starting gate. When he'd been extricated he set a scorching gallop, followed by Colliery Band, Kellsboro' Jack, Southern Hero, Forbra and Really True. Heartbreak Hill fell. Golden Miller was still standing at the water, despite a bad mistake.

Remus and Colliery Band led them into the country, where Delaneige and Pelorous Jack began to make headway. Golden Miller blundered at Becher's, and although he recovered cleverly, his confidence was shaken. At the Canal Turn he came down. Memories at once went back to Easter Hero; another spectacular Gold Cup winner to attempt the double and fail at this fence.

Delaneige and Pelorous Jack challenged Kellsboro' Jack and for three fences they jumped in line. Delaneige dropped back but the gigantic Pelorous Jack, ridden by W. Stott, held on to the last where he tried to drag his legs through the top. He came down heavily, leaving Dudley Williams on Kellsboro' Jack looking over a shoulder for the nearest danger.

The nearest was Really True, hard ridden by Mr. Frank Furlong but three lengths away at the finish. Slater was third, ridden by Mr. Michael Barry.

They were followed by Delaneige, Alpine Hut, Forbra, Trocadero, Southern Hero, Under Orders, Colliery Band, Egremont, Remus, Ruin, Near East, Trouble Maker, Ballybrack, Merriment and thirteen-year-old Shaun Goilin. Gregalach broke a blood vessel.

It was a popular victory for the American owner, Mrs. Florence Ambrose Clark. She and her husband were leading figures in the sporting world of America and had many friends in Britain. The decision which most endeared her to the Aintree crowd was her insistence that Kellsboro' Jack, although only seven, should not be risked over Aintree fences again. It might have deprived her son of Jackdaw from a second win or from joining the few who had won with top weight. It certainly saved him from the fate of Sergeant Murphy and Why Not and of many others who had been brought out year after year with depressing persistence.

Kellsboro' Jack was luckier than Golden Miller, the 'horse of the century' and his acknowledged conqueror at Cheltenham. Before the decade was out Golden Miller would be brought repeatedly to Aintree with a stubbornness which contrasted sharply with Mrs. Clark's compassion.

The year: 1934
Number of runners: Thirty
Winner: Golden Miller (G. Wilson—12 st 2 lb)
Time: 9 minutes 20⅖ seconds

The popular hero was Golden Miller, winner of twelve steeplechases, including three Gold Cups, with only one fall to blemish his record and that at the Canal the previous year. His supporters believed he could do what had never been done: win the Cheltenham race and the National in the same year. Such confirmation of versatility would establish him 'the horse of the century'.

Opinions were divided. Some experts doubted that he could get round, much less win. He jumped off his forehand, which made him vulnerable over drop fences. Moreover he did not seem the Aintree type, lacking the ruggedness of Manifesto. For weeks the experts argued, to be quoted in pubs and kitchens all over the land. But the public wanted him to win. A kind of mass will was behind him as he passed from the paddock to face his greatest test.

He had been trained to the minute by Basil Briscoe and his jockey was Gerry Wilson, son of a horse-dealer who had graduated from minor meetings and could say with a grin: 'I get paid for what I like doing best.' There was a great cheer for horse and jockey as they passed towards the starting tape.

Delaneige made the early running, followed at the water by Forbra, Gregalach, Remus, Golden Miller and the Whitney-owned Thomond II. Really True fell; Gregalach broke down; Thomond II was baulked by a loose horse yet still was not out of it. Approaching the last Delaneige was in front but the crowds were not watching Delaneige. They were looking beyond him to Golden Miller and Golden Miller was coming. The roar had relief in it.

Forbra and Thomond II were there with a chance. Delaneige had a length advantage over Golden Miller at the last, but the Cheltenham specialist proved his quality by quickening under 12 st 2 lb to show the stylishness of Easter Hero, the resolution of Cloister, the weight-carrying stamina of Manifesto. His victory by five lengths was incredible and had even his critics cheering.

Thomond II was third, five lengths behind Delaneige. Forbra was fourth, followed by Uncle Batt, Bachelor Prince, Apostasy and by Remus, the big horse who liked his pint.

The time was eight seconds faster than Kellsboro' Jack's record despite a weight of 12 st 2 lb compared with Kellsboro' Jack's 11 st 9 lb. It was a great triumph for Wilson, who had for years ridden with more pluck than luck.

While superlatives were being shouted by radio commentators and hammered out of typewriters by journalists, the Irish found consolation in the fact that 'the horse of the century' had been bred in Ireland by Mr. Lawrence Geraghty on a farm in Co. Meath. Sired by the modest stallion, Goldcourt, Golden Miller had been sold as a yearling at Dublin sales for a hundred guineas, but no one had thought much of him until Cambridgeshire trainer Basil Briscoe brought him to England, where he ran as a three-year-old over hurdles at Southwell.

He went on to steeplechasing and was narrowly beaten at Newbury, doing enough to persuade Mr. Philip Carr, father of Notts cricketer A. W. Carr, to buy him for £1,000. Mr. Carr died shortly afterwards and for £6,000 Golden Miller passed to Miss Dorothy Paget, eccentric daughter of Lord Queenborough and a formidable owner of steeplechasers. He won his first Gold Cup at five years old and was to win five in succession, three times beating Kellsboro' Jack to third place. But his taking of the National in record time was his greatest triumph.

The year: 1935
Number of runners: Twenty-seven
Winner: Reynoldstown (Mr. F. Furlong—11 st 4 lb)

Golden Miller, for the fourth time winner of the Cheltenham Gold Cup, came back to attempt another double. He carried a champion's weight of 12 st 7 lb, yet was everyone's choice at 2—1; the shortest favourite since odds-on Matthew in 1847. Four attendants surrounded him in the paddock like private detectives around a prince. He seemed to dwarf such horses as Thomond II, Royal Ransom, and Reynoldstown. The race promised to comprise Golden Miller and twenty-six others as Wilson rode him towards the start.

He jumped the early fences in brilliant fashion, but approaching Valentine's for the first time he seemed to gallop short, to think about refusal. Wilson wouldn't let him. He jumped reluctantly, screwing in his take-off and jolting Wilson from the saddle. It was an astonishing mistake. The crowds were still asking, 'Where is he? What happened?' as Thomond II led the survivors towards the water. Out of distressed bewilderment came the rumour that Golden Miller was another Zoedone, nobbled to save the bookmakers.

At Becher's for the second time Reynoldstown and the American-owned Thomond II were disputing the lead, followed by Castle Irwell, ridden by his American owner, Mr. G. H. Bostwick. Castle Irwell fell at the Canal and Reynoldstown went on from Thomond II, followed by Blue Prince and Lazy Boots.

Billy Speck rallied Thomond II and drove him to within half a length of Reynoldstown, but a hard race at Cheltenham, where he had been beaten only three-quarters of a length by Golden Miller, took its toll of Mr. Whitney's good horse.

Thomond II could find no more and the despairing Speck watched Reynoldstown, then Blue Prince, draw away.

Billy Parvin, another jockey to come up the hard way, forced Blue Prince to within three lengths despite a slipping saddle. Thomond II was third, eight lengths away. They were followed by Lazy Boots, Uncle Batt and Bachelor Prince.

The success of Reynoldstown, another to bear the name of his birthplace, gave the Irish plenty to celebrate. The seven-year-old was owned and trained by Major Noel Furlong who had come to Leicestershire from Co. Cork. Frank Furlong, until recently with the 9th Lancers, was his son, second on Really True two years previously.

Golden Miller was examined by veterinary surgeons and declared unharmed. He was brought out the following day for the Championship 'Chase; a decision which touched off a bomb of controversy. Many considered that in achieving the double he had done enough and that to persist at Aintree was to invite disaster. They were rebuked as sentimentalists, but were proved wiser than the experts.

Golden Miller had no heart for it. He reached the first fence and half-jumped, dislodging the unfortunate Wilson. The booing was the ugliest ever heard at Aintree. Some might have been booing from their pockets, but many were condemning more than jockey, trainer and owner. They were expressing judgment on all who in the past had destroyed good horses by asking too much, too often.

The immediate sequel was distasteful. Miss Paget took Golden Miller and six other steeplechasers from Briscoe's care and placed them with Donald Snow. A few months later Golden Miller passed on to Owen Anthony, with whom he remained for the rest of his career.

Briscoe moved to Royston and trained the Cambridgeshire winner Commander III, but those closest to him doubted that he ever got over the loss of Golden Miller. A few years later he gave up training and was almost forgotten by the racing community when he died in 1951.

The year: 1936
Number of runners: Thirty-five
Winner: Reynoldstown (Mr. F. Walwyn—12 st 2 lb)
Time: 9 minutes 37 seconds

Golden Miller, winner of his fifth Gold Cup, was back again, ridden by E. Williams. But now he seemed a lesser horse, diminished by scandalous rumours and public quarrels. Many believed he hated Aintree and that this hatred should be acknowledged and respected. Yet they backed him out of loyalty, their sympathies engaged in a manner which had not been possible before radio and news-reels and would not be repeated until television made Arkle a household name.

Avenger shared favouritism with Golden Miller, while Reynoldstown, carrying 12st 2 lb, had a different rider. Frank Furlong, bothered by increasing weight, offered the ride to Mr. Fulke Walwyn who had served with him in the 9th Lancers.

Among the extreme outsiders was Davy Jones, tubed reject from the flat, recently bought for £650 by the West Country peer, Lord Mildmay of Flete, for his son Anthony. At that time Anthony Mildmay was an inexperienced amateur with an ugly style and no great ability. But Devon families were on him to a man; partly out of regard for his father, partly in admiration of his courage.

A year before he had been almost killed in the Foxhunters' 'chase. The crashing fall might have been enough for most men, but long pain seemed only to make Anthony Mildmay more determined. He wanted to prove himself over fences and above all to win the National. His friend was Peter Cazalet at the Fairlawne stables where Harry Whiteman held the licence. Cazalet approved the purchase of Davy Jones from trainer Tom Rayner and was in the paddock as Mildmay mounted.

For some reason Mildmay did not tie his usual knot in the reins. This might have been nervous error. It might have been deliberate, since the absence of a knot would enable him to slip the reins when touching down over drop fences. The detail seemed to matter little, yet it was to cost Davy Jones the race and to deny Mildmay the spectacular achievement of a consuming ambition.

Golden Miller fell at the first and the sound from the stands was different from the usual lament for fallen money. There was anger in it and despair and a quality of I-told-you-so. Williams held on and remounted, but the 'horse of the century' was already far behind, ears flat and tail angry, telling everyone how he hated it. He continued to jump until the ditch after Valentine's, where he stiffened his forelegs and refused and kept on refusing, confirming what millions had guessed. His Aintree days were over. Only those closest to him seemed not to believe it.

Delaneige and Royal Ransom fell, leaving Davy Jones in front. The winner of two small races at Gatwick was a notorious puller and seemed to be running his own race. He passed the stands ahead of Avenger with Reynoldstown far back. The lead was increased when Avenger fell at the fence after the water, breaking his neck and shattering the hopes of his owner, Mrs. Mundy, who had been trying for forty years to win the National.

Over Becher's Davy Jones was still leading with Mildmay showing no sign of weakening. Walwyn had dropped his whip and had to punch Reynoldstown along with hands and heels. The 1935 winner responded gamely without narrowing the gap. At the ditch before the racecourse he jumped like a tired horse, dragging his back legs through and nearly falling. Walwyn held him up but Reynoldstown was feeling the weight, ominously slow in recovering his galloping rhythm. Neither trainer Furlong nor rider Walwyn could have given much for his chances.

Davy Jones seemed not to be extended and the West Country prepared to cheer its first victory in the National. Like all tubed horses, Davy Jones breathed 'like a grampus' and you could hear him breathing 'a mile away' as he hammered towards the second last. He jumped it well enough but pecked slightly on landing. Mildmay allowed the reins to slip to the buckle, giving him space to recover. It was the correct thing to do and only a composed amateur could have done it. But the prong of the buckle slipped through the hasp and suddenly the reins were flapping. Mildmay lost control. Davy Jones swerved and ran out, scattering spectators who didn't know what had happened.

Abruptly Reynoldstown was in front with nothing to beat; the luckiest winner since Ballymacad in 1917. Ego, whose dam in Ireland had been exchanged for a box of eggs, chased him home but could get no closer than twelve lengths. Bachelor Prince was third, six lengths away. Others to finish were Crown Prince, Inversible, Provocative, Castle Irwell, Double Crossed, Moorland View and Comedian.

Reynoldstown became the fifth to win the National twice and the third to win in successive years (excluding Poethlyn, one of whose victories was a wartime substitute at Gatwick). It was another triumph also for the 9th Lancers, which had produced good steeplechase riders as long ago as David Campbell.

The year: 1937
Number of runners: Thirty-three
Winner: Royal Mail (E. Williams—11 st 13 lb)
Time: 9 minutes 59½ seconds

It was centenary year; a time for looking back to William Lynn and Henry Potts and Captain Becher, for recalling the days when doctors followed the race on horse-back and when vast crowds came on foot to be robbed by thimble-riggers. But even in its year of celebration the National could not escape criticism.

The authorities decided to revert to a minimum weight of 10 st. Since 1931 the minimum had been 10 st 7 lb with the declared purpose of eliminating the mediocre. The measure, as one of several, had been largely successful. In 1934 there had been less than half the runners of 1929 and the result had been a genuine race, brilliantly won.

The decision to revert brought many protests, including a

published letter from former amateur George Lambton: 'The Grand National . . . is not meant to be won by moderate horses. . . . If the authorities encourage owners to enter them, the race will lose its high tone and quality and revert to the farcical scramble it became some years ago.'

There were other points of view. The public liked the race for its uncertainty. The most moderate horse could be 'in with a chance' as Tipperary Tim had proved. Moreover it cost no less to enter a bad horse than a good; the more bad horses, the more fees and forfeits to swell the final stake.

Reynoldstown did not try again, his owner, Major Furlong, observing that you can take 'the pitcher to the well too often'. There were no such scruples about Golden Miller. He came back despite his failures but with a different jockey. Danny Morgan succeeded Evan Williams and Gerry Wilson to the hot seat. An important absentee was Davy Jones, who had done everything except win the previous year. He developed leg trouble and could not be prepared for the race.

King George VI and Queen Elizabeth were there to watch Ready Cash lead the field over Becher's for the first time. Golden Miller was moving smoothly until he reached the fatal open ditch. He refused again, showing a stubbornness similar to Fan and Arravale in other years.

Delaneige became involved in a mix-up and Fred Rimell, son of the trainer of Forbra, was clouted out of the saddle. Ego, Cooleen and Pucka Belle were prominent as they passed the stands. Royal Mail, black son of My Prince and trained by Ivor Anthony, was lying handy.

At the fourth fence on the second circuit Evan Williams let Royal Mail go on, followed by Mr. J. V. Rank's Cooleen, ridden by Jack Fawcus, and by Pucka Belle, owned and ridden by Mr. Eric Bailey. They continued in that order over Becher's, where Cooleen was badly hampered by the loose horse Drin. Fawcus fought him off, but Drin came at the mare and tried to savage her.

Royal Mail, escaping the confusion, lengthened his lead three out to win comfortably from Cooleen. The point-to-point mare

Pucka Belle was third, followed by Crown Prince, Pencraik and Don Bradman.

It was a second winner for Ivor Anthony, who had produced Kellsboro' Jack to win in 1933. But it was the sixth win for the Wroughton stable, since its former occupant, the Hon. Aubrey Hastings, had trained Ascetic's Silver, Ally Sloper, Master Robert and the Gatwick winner, Ballymacad.

Royal Mail was owned by Mr. Hugh Lloyd Thomas, formerly assistant secretary to the Prince of Wales (who became the Duke of Windsor) and a member of the British Embassy in Paris. The last of My Prince's three National winners, Royal Mail had been bred by Mr. C. Rogers in Ireland and sold as a three-year-old to Mr. Hubert Hartigan, from whom Mr. Thomas had bought him.

Evan Williams, luckier on Royal Mail than he had been on Golden Miller, was a former amateur who had carried out secretarial duties at the Wroughton stable. He turned professional and after a successful riding career, trained for the flat at Kingsclere. Later he became a master of fox-hounds in Ireland, where his wife owned the Knockaney Stud in Co. Limerick.

The year: 1938
Number of runners: Thirty-six
Winner: Battleship (B. Hobbs—11 st 6 lb)
Time: 9 minutes 29⅘ seconds

Thirty years had passed since the American-bred Rubio had won for Major Pennant; fifteen since the American-owned Sergeant Murphy had won for Stephen Sandford; twelve since Jack Horner had repaid his price in a fortnight; five since Kellsboro' Jack had won for Mrs. Clark. Through three decades dollar fortunes had been spent on the search for winners. Billy Barton, Easter Hero and Thomond II had failed. So had the Pennsylvanian hunter, Glangesia. Success came unexpectedly with a pony stallion, at 15.2 hands the smallest winner since The Lamb in 1871 and ridden by the youngest jockey in the history of the race.

During the parade Battleship was more a curiosity than a serious contender. The blinkered son of Man O' War looked overwhelmed by the powerful Royal Danieli; his seventeen-year-old jockey, Bruce Hobbs, looked a schoolboy. They seemed a small partnership for such an ordeal. Even Americans hesitated to back their contender and bookmakers were offering 40—1 as Battleship went to the start.

It promised to be a one-horse race as Royal Danieli strode in front with a stylish confidence reminiscent of Easter Hero. Only Workman and Battleship could stay with him and at Becher's for the second time the little American began to take on the giant Royal Danieli. Workman was about five lengths behind.

So far the pony, owned by Mrs. Marion Scott and trained by Reg Hobbs, had jumped everything with courage and skill. So far the young jockey, coached by his father, had shown the determined calm of a veteran. But three fences out their luck seemed to explode. Battleship made his only mistake. He was almost down and Mrs. Scott must have thought her chance lost. But Bruce Hobbs rallied him and kept him going. When Workman blundered, Battleship seemed sure of second place. That was all Americans could hope for. Even that seemed achievement enough as Battleship approached the last.

Royal Danieli jumped it two lengths in front and Dan Moore could choose his ground. He claimed the rails. Hobbs had the centre of the course, which David Campbell had long ago declared to be the best. They fought it out stride for stride while the sympathies of the crowd switched from the well-backed Royal Danieli to the youngest on the smallest. With a hundred yards remaining the Americans still did not visualise victory. They were ready to settle for gallant defeat. But Battleship had the courage of a giant. He gave all he had and was still half a length behind. He reached for the dregs and found something more and was in front for the first time in the last stride.

Dan Moore thought Royal Danieli had won and the Irish thought he was right. There was long delay before the official verdict was given. Or perhaps it only seemed long delay.

Certainly the packed crowd stood in absolute silence while seconds ticked as slowly as the traditional silence of Armistice Day.

When the judge declared Battleship the winner, the tension erupted in Irish fury and American delight. Bookmakers shared the jubilation, for Battleship had been so little supported that only one had backed him in the first leg of the Tote double. The holder of the 10*s* ticket was Lord Digby and he won £5,000.

Workman was third. Others to finish were Cooleen, Delachance, Red Knight, Blue Shirt, Under Bid, Hopeful Hero, Bachelor Prince, Lough Cottage, Provocative and Drin. Battleship did not appear at Aintree again. He went back to America and a hero's reception.

The year: 1939
Number of runners: Thirty-seven
Winner: Workman (T. Hyde—10 st 6 lb)
Time: 9 minutes $42\frac{1}{5}$ seconds

It was a fateful year in European history, but the crowds at Aintree clung to the hope that by some alchemy of international politics, war would be averted. Newspapers which gave their front pages to Hitler and Neville Chamberlain gave their sports pages to the National. Kilstar, owned by Miss Paget and rumoured to be another Golden Miller, was the popular tip. But on the course the 'whisper' was for Workman, third the previous year and owned by Sir Alexander Maguire, formerly of Liverpool with business interests in Dublin.

In the Sefton Arms you could hear Irish whispers that Dublin had 'its shirt on'. If you asked about Royal Danieli, so narrowly beaten in 1938, you were told that his feet had 'gone wrong' and that he might have to run without plates. Only the bravest Scot, surrounded by the Irish, dared mention MacMoffat, the £60 hunter, owned by Captain L. Scott Briggs and ridden by Ben Alder.

Kilstar, ridden by George Archibald, was always prominent

on the first circuit but Royal Danieli fell at Becher's. Kilstar took the water confidently and continued to jump without hesitation or error until Becher's for the second time. He blundered heavily and dropped with legs spread-eagled. For a moment he seemed to be down and Archibald heard him groan. Then he dragged himself erect and tried to come again. But twenty lengths had been lost and Workman was 'away', followed by Black Hawk.

The most formidable thing about Black Hawk was Jack Moloney, second three times, once fourth and determined to win at last. He drove Black Hawk level with Workman and they jumped the last together. They bumped in mid-air. Black Hawk got the worst of it and toppled, crashing down with Moloney, ambition and all. Workman went on alone but began to look around in the fashion of a horse left suddenly in front. He was almost surprised by MacMoffat as the Scot came from 'nowhere' to put in a brave challenge. But Workman quickened to win by three lengths, with Kilstar fifteen lengths third.

They were followed by Cooleen, Symaethis, Dominick's Cross, West Point, Pencraik and the 1937 winner, Royal Mail. Gerry Wilson, who had ridden Golden Miller, got round on Under Bid to finish tenth.

The Irish had the band out for Workman when he returned to the land where good horses come from. It was almost like the good old days of Empress and The Liberator, of Frigate and Troytown. There were cheers to spare for Tim Hyde, the show-ring rider who had turned steeplechase jockey at the suggestion of trainer John Ruttle because 'only Hyde was right for Workman'.

More than a decade was ending. An era of cruel contrasts was ending too. The 1920s had been years of industrial strife and strikes and bitter poverty, of champagne in slippers and frenetic gaiety. The 1930s had proved years of repression through unemployment, of fear and soup kitchens and crooners and whoopee and an actress insuring her legs for a million dollars. Suddenly it was over, but it did not seem to be over.

Even a declaration of war on September 3rd, 1939, changed little. Three months after the beginning of the biggest war in history, horses were being prepared for the Grand National of 1940.

13

It was a crazy war. It refused to start. The British Expeditionary Force was in France but nothing seemed to be happening. The newspapers had so little to report about the war on land, at sea and in the air, that they gave their usual space to the big steeplechase of the year.

On 'National Friday' the only hints of war were barrage balloons lying bloated in the sky above Merseyside and uniforms looking new and conspicuous among the crowds.

The year: 1940
Number of runners: Thirty
Winner: Bogskar (M. A. Jones—10 st 4 lb)
Time: 9 minutes 20$\frac{3}{5}$ seconds

A major condition was that riders must have won five steeplechases under recognised rules in any country. In the past this would have excluded some amateurs who seemed totally inexperienced yet who contrived to succeed where professionals failed. It was part of a gradual process of change, the emphasis passing from 'riding for fun' to the benefit of professionals, who had felt for years that they were too often excluded from the biggest steeplechase by 'mad amateurs' seeking glory.

Royal Danieli was favourite, with plenty of support for Miss Paget's Kilstar, Milano and the Scottish hope, MacMoffat.

Venturesome Knight was ridden by Mr. Reg Tweedie, for ten years a leading amateur in the Border country and the friendly rival of another Northern amateur, Mr. Alec Marsh.

Royal Danieli set a fast pace but at the water Bogskar, MacMoffat and Gold Arrow were well placed. It had become a maxim among National riders that to be 'in the first twelve at the water' was essential. On the second circuit the riderless National Knight began to harass the leaders. Royal Danieli was fading and MacMoffat, again ridden by Alder, took it up, followed by Bogskar, Gold Arrow and Venturesome Knight.

Royal Danieli fell heavily and could not get up for a long time. He had wrenched his shoulder muscles so badly that he never raced again. Meanwhile MacMoffat was trying to shake off the loose horse and the effort probably cost him the race. He was still in front at the last, raising hopes for the first-ever Scottish victory, but Bogskar was coming fast. They jumped it together. Bogskar made a slight mistake, then recovered strongly to draw away in a time only fractionally outside Golden Miller's record.

MacMoffat was second, Gold Arrow third. Venturesome Knight broke a blood vessel, splashing Reg Tweedie's knees with blood. Yet he still finished fourth. Lazy Boots got round, ridden by Sir Geoffrey Congreve who was with the Royal Navy and had a naval beard. Others to finish were Professor II, Takvor Pasha, Inversible, Away, Dominick's Cross, Kilstar, Luxborough, Rockquilla, Downright, Tuckmill and Red Eagle.

Bogskar was owned by Lord Stalbridge, a member of the National Hunt Committee who trained his own steeplechasers at Eastbury with the help of ex-jockey Jack Kelly. Lord Stalbridge is officially credited with the training, which makes him the first peer to owner-train a National winner.

The unluckiest professional of the year was Eric Foley, who missed the ride because of injury. Mervyn Jones, a nephew of Ivor Anthony and serving as a Pilot-Sergeant with the R.A.F., was his deputy. Two years later Jones was killed in action.

The years: 1941–5

The sluggish war erupted and the sky above Aintree was full of flames. The Grand National was abandoned, although racing continued elsewhere and the Gold Cup was held at Cheltenham in 1941 and 1942. No attempt was made to transfer the National to another course.

By 1942 the national effort had intensified to 'total war'. Grasslands were ploughed to produce food. Every patch of ground, including the marginal yards beside railway embankments, had to be made productive on the slogan 'Dig for Victory'. It was good sense, but horses couldn't be kept without grass.

In the rural counties farmers had to dispose of old horses, young horses, brood mares, although somehow they contrived to keep a few favourites. A source which had supplied steeplechasing for more than a hundred years was virtually closed and by 1943 a thoroughbred was a liability, so demanding was it of time and grass.

Many good horses were lost in the war years. Those who had been seven years old in 1939, on the edge of their prime and promising great things, were becoming old and stiff and beyond recovery. The big names of 1939 were already dead or pensioned off.

Good jockeys were lost, also. Some, including Frank Furlong who had won on Reynoldstown, were killed on active service. Others lost vital years in the sands of the Middle East and the jungles of the Far East. By the time war was over potential champions in 1939 were almost forgotten while those who had been schoolboys were knocking for places in the limelight.

The war ended in 1945 and work began to restore Aintree as the centre of steeplechasing. The mood was high, all optimism and impatience. Crowds rushed to Aintree for the first post-war National with an enthusiasm equal to any of the great years. Yet something had happened, not only to the National but to all the big events which had seemed worth preserving intact. Nothing would ever be quite the same again.

The year: 1946
Number of runners: Thirty-four
Winner: Lovely Cottage (Captain R. Petre—10 st 8 lb)
Time: 9 minutes 38⅕ seconds

It was the year Prince Regent came to Aintree. Already eleven years old, his best years lost in wartime obscurity, he had a massive reputation and a weight to match. The handicapper awarded him 12 st 5 lb. Trainer Tom Dreaper judged him the best horse in Ireland. Jockey Tim Hyde, who had come from the show-ring to win on Workman, would not hear of defeat. The experts thought Prince Regent capable of giving 25 lb to Lovely Cottage.

How good Lovely Cottage was may be judged by the fact that he'd been advertised for sale at £2,000 plus £1,000 'when he wins a Grand National'. Mr. John Morant had paid the price and accepted the contingency, sending the eight-year-old to Tommy Rayson. How good Prince Regent was may be judged from the fact that he almost pulled it off.

Throughout the first circuit he promised to justify all hopes and boasts, lying handy to Limestone Edward and dominating the rest in a fashion reminiscent of Troytown. The packed stands cheered him over the water, then cheered again as he took over from Limestone Edward. By now the course was littered with the fallen. Loose horses were lolloping, seeking ways out. They ran beside Prince Regent. They nagged him and checked him and crossed him. Hyde had to shake them off as Alder had tried to shake off National Knight when MacMoffat might have won.

Hyde rode what amounted to a series of finishes, yet still Prince Regent was in front. He reached the last fence to the old cry, 'He's only got to stand up to win.' He stood up, yet still he did not win.

His ears were flopping, his nostrils flew tattered banners. His head went down in weariness and although he went on giving, dredging up the dregs in the fashion of a great horse who will not consider defeat, he could not hold off Lovely Cottage.

Hyde saw Captain Petre's cap go by, then the back of the Captain's colours. The sound from the stands was alight with dismay and affection. The crowds weren't watching the winner. They were scarcely aware that Jack Finlay had stolen second place. They were watching the beaten favourite, calling him home with an admiring roar which made it seem like victory.

Lovely Cottage won by four lengths from Jack Finlay with Prince Regent an exhausted third. Captain Petre, thirty-three years old and until recently with the Scots Guards, was the last amateur to ride the winner for nineteen years.

Only three others got round. They were Housewarmer, Schubert and Limestone Edward. Symbole was killed at Becher's. The twenty-six others who failed to finish were Red Rower, Largo, Heirdom, Bogskar, Kami, MacMoffat, Astrometer, Knight's Crest, Suzerain II, E.P., Vain Knight, Newark Hill, Silver Flame, Historical Revue, Tulyra, Dunshaughlin, Double Flash, Yung Yat, King Gesson, Lough Conn, Musical Lad, Bricett, Gyppo, Alacrity, Closure and Elsich.

The year: 1947
Number of runners: Fifty-seven
Winner: Caughoo (E. Dempsey—10 st)
Time: 10 minutes $3\frac{1}{5}$ seconds

At the request of Clement Attlee's Government the race was held on a Saturday. It was the biggest field since 1929 and the second biggest in 110 years. The going was all mud. Weeks of snow and frost were followed by relentless rain. Training schedules were interrupted. Preliminary races were cancelled. Any fully fit horse must have a chance. Conditions were right for another fluke and Caughoo was it at 100—1.

Prince Regent, with 12 st 7 lb, was back and the public responded by making him favourite. Mr. J. V. Rank's horse had succeeded Golden Miller in popular regard and eighteen years would pass at Aintree before another was accorded such affection. First of the Dandies was trying again. So were fourteen-year-old Bogskar and fifteen-year-old MacMoffat.

From the stands only part of the course could be seen and spectators on the far side, huddled near Becher's and Valentine's, relied on portable radios and Raymond Glendenning to tell them what was happening. Revelry and E.P. fell at the first, Bullington and Michael's Pearl at the third where Prince Regent blundered but kept his feet. Day Dreams was pulled up as they approached Becher's for the first time. Linthill dropped out. The fallers included Tribune, Oh Joe, Bogskar, MacMoffat, First of the Dandies, Gyppo, Parthenon, Prattler, Border Bob, Black Jennifer, Klaxton, Good Date, Shanakill, Bomber Command and Martin M. Grecian Victory was brought down. So were Bricett, Luan Cassa, Musical Lad and Sheila's Cottage.

Prince Regent was there with a chance as they jumped Becher's for the second time, but after that he struggled in the mud. Caughoo, with a weight advantage of 25 lb, went on with another Irish light-weight, Lough Conn. Silver Flame, ridden by Captain Petre, was in a challenging position three out, where he was impeded and brought down by Tulyra. Soda II fell. Yung-Yat and Domino dropped out.

Caughoo jumped the last in front while rain-drenched spectators tried to identify his colours and to guess his name. They were still guessing as he ran home twenty lengths in front of the eleven-year-old Lough Conn. At the last Prince Regent promised to be third for the second time, but Kami, ridden by amateur John Hislop, showed no mercy to the weary favourite, squeezing him out of third place.

Others to finish were Housewarmer, Refugio, Kilanglory, Clyduffe, Oculator, Toyette, Halcyon Hours, Brick Bat, Schubert, Leap Man, Brighter Sandy, Rowland Roy, Rearmament and Handy Lad.

Caughoo, the third 100—1 winner, was owned and trained by the brothers J. and H. McDowell. He had won two Ulster Grand Nationals and had never fallen. More important he'd had the luck to be prepared on Portmarnock sands, far from the snow and mud which had frustrated English trainers.

The year: 1948
Number of runners: Forty-three
Winner: Sheila's Cottage (A. P. Thompson—10 st 7 lb)
Time: 9 minutes $24\frac{4}{5}$ seconds

It was another year for the Irish but it should have been Lord Mildmay's. Anthony Mildmay had inherited the title Lord Mildmay of Flete and after war service with the Welsh Guards and Guards Armoured Division, had come back to England determined to establish a string of useful steeplechasers. His partner was Peter Cazalet. Their stables were at Fairlawne in Kent. Their shared ambition was to win the National with Mildmay riding.

For two years the public had given Mildmay growing support as he rode at big meetings and small. They remembered his hard-luck defeat on Davy Jones and respected his courageous dedication. Moreover they recognised him to be a genuine amateur, representing the best of the past in a society racked by change. Like Lord Coventry eighty years before, he was superior to and remote from the grubby trickery to which the sport was vulnerable. The maxim was: 'When you're on m'Lord you're on a trier.' There can have been few who tried harder.

His favourite horse was Cromwell, seven years old and handicapped at 10 st 11 lb. Again the West Country was on him, as fervent about the partnership of Mildmay-Cromwell as Cheltenham had been for Stevens and The Colonel or Yorkshire for the Poethlyn-Piggott combination.

'The Regent' was there again, thirteen years old yet still formidable. He was to fail again, yet even his failure was to be a kind of triumph. It was because of what happened to Prince Regent under heavy burdens that owners and trainers of other good horses learned a belated lesson. In 1933 Mrs. Clark had refused to allow Kellsboro' Jack to be entered for another National; in 1937 Major Furlong had refused to take Reynoldstown 'to the well too often'. After 'The Regent's' noble failures others showed a charity to their horses which would have been condemned sentimental weakness fifty years before.

Mildmay's luck began to give out before the race began. Cromwell was kicked during the line-up and took a long time to recover. During the first circuit, with First of the Dandies the bold front-runner, he jumped sluggishly, so far back at the water that he seemed to have no chance.

The favourite, Silver Flame, was already gone, unluckily brought down at Becher's. Bricett, Cloncarrig, Sir John, Tudor Close, Ulster Monarch, Loyal Antrim, Ultra Bene, Some Chicken, Bora's Cottage and Tommy Traddles were among the early fallers.

First of the Dandies, confidently ridden by J. Brogan and lightly weighted with 10 st 4 lb, turned into the country, followed by Rowland Roy, Parthenon, Maltese Wanderer, Happy Home and Prince Regent. During the third mile Cromwell improved steadily, reaching Becher's in the leading group and apparently full of steam. It was then that Mildmay's luck ran dry.

Several months before he had broken his neck at Folkestone, since when he had been afflicted by sudden cramps in the muscles of his neck. It had happened before during a minor race and had mattered little. It happened again with a mile remaining. Unable to raise his head, Mildmay could not see more than a few yards. He could only sit motionless, chin on chest in an attitude of despair.

He seemed to have given up. Many in the crowd were bewildered. Aware of his dedication, they wondered why he did not ride with the determination of Eddie Reavey on Zahia, Arthur Thompson on Sheila's Cottage, Brogan on First of the Dandies and Gene Kelly on Happy Home. Only his friends guessed and suffered with him as he rode 'blind', leaving it to the horse. It was a memorable feat of courage, but it could not be enough.

First of the Dandies went on to the last while—unknown to Mildmay—another tragedy was being acted out behind. Zahia jumped the second last full of running and seemed certain to catch the pace-maker. Suddenly he ran out, as abruptly as Davy Jones in 1936. Not until later was it clear that jockey Reavey had misunderstood the peculiarities of the run-in; going right of the water jump and squandering the chance of a lifetime. Later he was to mourn: 'I was only cantering—I must have won, no question.' But great races are not won by hard luck stories. Both Mildmay and Reavey shared the might-have-been while First of the Dandies continued towards apparently certain victory.

Yet still the surprises were not over. Trained by Gerry Wilson, who had won on Golden Miller in 1934, First of the Dandies was 'out on his feet'. As long as there was a fence to challenge him, his spirit responded; but after the last he saw only the punishing climb to the finish. His courage wilted, his stride shortened. He tried to hang on as Sheila's Cottage came alongside.

From that point it was a long duel between Brogan and Arthur Thompson, worthy of comparison with the great battles of the past. Fifty yards out Sheila's Cottage got her head in front and went on to win by a length. The hat which rose first and highest was trainer Neville Crump's.

At 50—1 Sheila's Cottage was his first National winner and the third to be sired by Cottage. It was a first success also for jockey Thompson, a tall Irishman whose tactics were exactly opposite to the waiting game which George Stevens had perfected in the nineteenth century. Thompson liked to be in front, sure that the best way to avoid trouble was to be ahead of it.

Cromwell finished an honourable third, only six lengths behind First of the Dandies despite Mildmay's inability to see. Happy Home was fourth, followed by Platypus, Rowland Roy, Parthenon, Maltese Wanderer, Offaly Prince, Klaxton, War Risk, Revelry, Schubert and Lovely Cottage.

Prince Regent was carried out at the twenty-third fence where Caughoo was pulled up. Lough Conn broke a blood vessel. The prize to the winner was £9,103.

The year: 1949
Number of runners: Forty-three
Winner: Russian Hero (L. McMorrow—10 st 8 lb)
Time: 9 minutes 23$\frac{4}{5}$ seconds

It was a fateful year in the history of the Grand National. Lord Sefton sold the site which his family had owned for generations. It was bought by Messrs. Topham, members of which family had been associated with the race almost from its inception. But the future of the National seemed guaranteed by a covenant, imposed by Lord Sefton, that the land should not be used for 'purposes other than racing or agriculture'.

Cromwell, at eight years old, was 6—1 favourite, again ridden by Lord Mildmay. But there was plenty of support for Happy Home, fourth the previous year, owned by Miss Paget and trained by Fulke Walwyn, who had won on Reynoldstown in 1936. In the pre-race parade none paid much attention to Russian Hero, a nine-year-old who had fallen last time out and had shown no ability to stay more than three miles.

Parthenon slipped up at the first fence and Sagacity fell at the second. Caughoo was pulled up at the fifth. The early fallers included Cloncarrig, Cavaliero, Caddie II, Magnetic Fin, Arranbeg, Replica, Martin M, Stone Cottage, Morning Star II, Ship's Bell, Offaly Prince and Barn Dance.

Monaveen, trained by Cazalet and ridden by Tony Grantham, led on the second circuit but fell at the nineteenth. Wot No Sun, Southborough, Bruno II, Royal Antrim, and Bora's Cottage disappeared. There was a mix-up at the Canal Turn where Brighter Sandy, Ulster Monarch and Sen Toi were brought down. There was more confusion three out, where Astra, ridden by Arthur Thompson, was baulked and Gallery was brought down. Cromwell was still there with a chance, although harassed by loose horses.

As the leaders reached the racecourse Roimond promised to win for Lord Bicester, whose black, gold and red colours were famous in steeplechasing yet who was destined never to win a National. But Russian Hero, trained in Cheshire by George

Owen, was going the better, regardless of form and the derision of the morning papers. Larry McMorrow kept him in front at the last and the nine-year-old, never to show such form again in a long series of races, stayed the distance easily to win by eight lengths.

Roimond, ridden by Dick Francis, was second and Royal Mount third. Cromwell was fourth, followed by Flaming Steel. Happy Home was sixth despite a bad mistake at Valentine's.

Others to finish were Tonderman, Lucky Purchase, Bricett, Clyduffe and Perfect Night.

A decade torn by war was over. Another was to begin which would see the emergence of Queen Elizabeth as an owner of top-class steeplechasers. Her interest had been stimulated by Lord Mildmay and her first steeplechaser was Monaveen; a faller in the 1949 race, bought for her by Peter Cazalet and due to run in Royal colours in 1950.

14

The year: 1950
Number of runners: Forty-nine
Winner: Freebooter (J. Power—11 st 11 lb)
Time: 9 minutes 23$\frac{3}{5}$ seconds

The previous year Monaveen had been a nonentity, 50—1 in the betting. Since then he had been bought by Queen Elizabeth, who shared ownership as she shared her love of horses with her elder daughter, Princess Elizabeth. It was in the Princess's colours that Monaveen ran in his second National; the first time Royal colours had been carried since the death of King Edward VII in 1910.

The race was memorable for another reason; it was Lord Mildmay's last attempt to achieve his ambition. He was forty years old, well beyond the age when many steeplechase amateurs elect to retire. But there was no mention of imminent retirement as he prepared to ride Cromwell for the third time. Fate was to be crueller than that.

Roimond, Cloncarrig and Rowland Roy were in the big field, while there was a tip on the day for Shagreen, ridden by Gene Kelly.

The race began badly at the first fence. Zarter was brought down as Cottage Welcome, Skouras and Comeragh fell. Russian Hero, doing what had been predicted for him the previous year,

Troytown (J. Anthony), formidable winner of 1920

The first fence in 1965. Freddie, in his first National, leads the field (extreme right)

Bogskar (M. A. Jones) leads MacMoffat over the last in 1940. The Scottish horse suffered some interference from the riderless horse

Kapeno leads at the Chair in the National of 1966, followed by Freddie on the inside, Norther, the blinkered L'Empereur, and Loving Record

The finish of all-time—Bryan Marshall gets Royal Tan home from Tudor Line (G. Slack) in 1954

toppled with them. Tommy Traddles was also down.

As the leaders came away from the débâcle the stands looked for the joint favourites, Freebooter and Roimond. They were safe. So was Monaveen. The radio commentator tried to pick out the colours as they approached the second, where Ivan's Choice came down. Cavaliero went at Becher's. So did Battling Pedulas, Gallery and Ardnacassa. Roimond fell when on the heels of Monaveen.

At the end of the first circuit the course was littered with the fallen and the race was reduced to a handful. The stands looked in vain for Lord Mildmay's cap. His luck had struck again at the eleventh, where Cromwell had been brought down. Garde Toi had had also gone, brought down at the eighth with the Marquis de Portago. Among the missing were Happy Rover, Cadamstown, Knockirr, Southborough, Stockman, Royal Mount, Castledermot, Inverlochy, Barney VI, Possible, San Michele, Highland Cottage, Limestone Cottage and Pastime. Monaveen had made a bad mistake at the fourteenth but was still there with a chance as Cloncarrig, Freebooter, Shagreen, Saintfield and Achton Major led the survivors towards Becher's for the second time.

Angel Hill, ridden by T. Shone, went into the lead and looked like running away with it until he hit the Canal fence. Shagreen fell, leaving Cloncarrig in front, followed by Freebooter. As they took the long bend from Valentine's towards the second last, Cloncarrig seemed to be moving smoothly. But over his right shoulder Bob Turnell heard the come-on of hooves and out of the corner of his eye saw Power on Freebooter. Cloncarrig tried to respond but misjudged his jump, hit the second last and stood on his nose.

Freebooter had nothing to beat. He came home an easy winner, followed by Arthur Thompson on Wot No Sun and by R. J. O'Ryan on Achton Major. The distances were fifteen lengths and ten lengths; but those who extolled Freebooter as an outstanding horse were surprised to find that his official time was only fractionally faster than that recorded by Russian Hero the previous year.

Freebooter was a son of Steel Point and bred in Co. Waterford. Bought as an unbroken three-year-old for 620 guineas, he had passed to Mrs. L. Brotherton two years later, by which time the price had risen to 3,000 gns. He was trained by Aintree-specialist Bobby Renton, who saddled the winners of every steeplechase at Aintree during more than fifty years of training. When he was over seventy, he still liked to ride one race a season.

The Lord Mildmay story ended on May 12th, 1950. He left his Mothecombe home to go down to the beach for a morning bathe. He was never seen alive again. Presumably he was a victim of the sudden cramp which had deprived him of the National in 1948. *The Times* said of him: 'There never was a harder rider, a better loser, or a more popular winner.' Tormented by pain and frustrated by injury, he had been denied the realisation of his governing ambition, yet he won the greatest victory of all; achieving what *The Times* described as 'a kind of immortality among the English'.

The year: 1951
Number of runners: Thirty-six
Winner: Nickel Coin (J. Bullock—10 st 1 lb)
Time: 9 minutes 47⅖ seconds

It wasn't a race. It was a shambles. The starter pressed his lever while many of the horses were still walking around. Jockeys were adjusting caps and reins. Some were checking their girths. They heard the rattle-up of the tape, the incredulous wail from the stands. They turned their horses as best they could and set off in pursuit. Freebooter and Cloncarrig were among them.

There seemed to be no provision for recall; no attempt to rectify the most ghastly mistake in the history of the race. Owners who had spent considerable sums preparing their horses; trainers who had spent months; thousands who had travelled long distances; all were united in a roar of protest which sounded like disgust.

Fiasco became tragedy at the first fence. Twelve horses came down or were brought down. The mêlée was without precedent. Jockeys made themselves as small as pheasants in long grass, waiting for danger to miss them. Horses floundered and struggled up, looking for a way out. In effect the race ended there and during those minutes something happened to the prestige of the Grand National. There was a feeling among those within the sport and outside it that such a mess couldn't have happened elsewhere. Blunder and confusion became associated with Aintree from that day.

Arctic Gold led the survivors over Becher's and continued in front to the Canal Turn, where he brought down Cloncarrig and three others. Out of the scramble came Russian Hero and Dog Watch, both trained by George Owen and doomed to come down at the Chair. With more than two miles remaining, the race was a dismal procession.

Soon only two were left: Nickel Coin, ridden by Bullock, and Royal Tan, ridden by Mr. O'Brien. They were together from Becher's to Valentine's and continued as close as brothers until the last, where Royal Tan made a bad mistake. Mr. O'Brien clung to his neck and struggled back, but Nickel Coin could not be caught. Derrinstown was remounted to finish third.

Nickel Coin was owned by Mr. J. Royle and trained by Jack O'Donoghue. The mare had begun as a show-jumper, and had finished second to that patriarch of show-jumping, Foxhunter.

Those who did not complete the course were Freebooter, Shagreen, Cloncarrig, Finnure, Roimond, Land Fort, Russian Hero, Arctic Gold, Sergeant Kelly, Rowland Roy, Prince Brownie, Armoured Knight, Stalbridge Rock, Cadamstown, Galley, East A'Calling, Stockman, Parpoint, Dog Watch, Broomfield, Texas Dan, Irish Lizard, Glen Fire, Binghamstown, Caesar's Wife, Parsonshill, Gay Heather, Column, Tasman, Queen of the Dandies, Revealed, Confucius, and Morning Cover.

The year: 1952
Number of runners: Forty-seven
Winner: Teal (A. P. Thompson—10 st 12 lb)
Time: 9 minutes 20$\frac{3}{5}$ seconds

After 1951 came fiasco of another kind. The Aintree executive and the B.B.C. were involved in a dispute over copyright. The deadlock could not be resolved and the Topham administration substituted its own broadcast for the highly efficient commentary which the B.B.C. had relayed since 1927.

The result infuriated those who listened. Little could be understood. Such muddle would never be forgotten, perhaps never forgiven. Abruptly 'The Grand' race seemed a joke, a travesty, and the prestige of the Grand National, already dented by the shambles of 1951, suffered another blow.

Again there was chaos at the first. Russian Hero, now twelve years old, disappeared with Golden Surprise, High Venture, St. Kathleen II, Dominick's Bar, Rocket VI, Cardinal Error, Irish Lizard, Court Painter and future winner Early Mist. Before the eighth, Cream of the Border, Kelek, Whispering Steel, Bronze Arrow, Caesar's Wife, Inter Alia, Cloncarrig, Niagara, Skouras, Wolfschmidt, Skyreholme, Pearly Prince and Tantivity were also gone.

Only eighteen were standing at the end of the first circuit. Freebooter, Royal Tan, Teal, Legal Joy and Wot No Sun were among them. So were Roimond, Derrinstown, and Icy Calm ridden by the Marquis de Portago.

The former point-to-pointer Teal went on at a good gallop, chased by Freebooter and Royal Tan. Freebooter fell at the Canal Turn, from which point it became a race between Teal, Legal Joy and Royal Tan. Again Mr. O'Brien's good horse faltered at the last, falling heavily when about to challenge.

Teal drew away from Legal Joy to win by five lengths. It was a second National for trainer Crump and a second for Arthur Thompson. Michael Scudamore, a product of point-to-pointing, was 'in the National frame' for the first time, followed by Dave Dick on Wot No Sun.

Others to get round were Uncle Barney, Overshadow, Printers Pie, Hierba, Column and Parsonshill.

Teal was owned by Mr. H. Lane and had begun as a hunter, qualifying for point-to-points and proving himself a jumping stayer of the highest class. The following year he was found to have a twisted gut. A major operation could not repair it and before the National of 1953 he had to be destroyed.

The year: 1953
Number of runners: Thirty-two
Winner: Early Mist (B. Marshall—11 st 2 lb)
Time: 9 minutes 21⅖ seconds

In the absence of Royal Tan, Vincent O'Brien's powerful stable at Cashel, Co. Tipperary, was represented by Early Mist; an English-bred eight-year-old, originally bought by Mr. H. Bonner on behalf of Mr. J. V. Rank, who had owned Prince Regent and had tried for years to win a National.

Early Mist had carried Mr. Rank's hopes and colours in 1952, but had fallen at the first when ridden by Pat Taaffe. Shortly afterwards Mr. Rank died and his horses came up for disposal.

Vincent O'Brien attended the sale and bought Early Mist for 5,300 guineas on behalf of Mr. J. Griffin. Ironically the under-bidder was Lord Bicester, who had also owned good horses in the hope of winning a National. Mr. Griffin already owned Royal Tan and, following his purchase of Early Mist, was to win with both; achieving twice in successive years what neither Lord Bicester nor Mr. Rank had been able to achieve in all their years of endeavour. In Ireland they called it 'the luck of Mincemeat Joe'.

Little Yid, ridden by J. Power who had won on Freebooter in 1950, was 7—1 favourite; while there was plenty of support for Whispering Steel, Glen Fire and Mont Tremblant, winner if the 1952 Gold Cup and owned by Miss Paget.

Grand Truce and Quite Naturally, ridden by Tim Molony, came down at the first, but the smaller field reduced the risks of early chaos. Arthur Thompson was unlucky at the eleventh, where Larry Fin was brought down as Glen Fire and Punchestown Star refused.

Ordnance, ridden by Scudamore, set a strong gallop on the second circuit, followed by Mont Tremblant, Early Mist, Little Yid, Irish Lizard, Overshadow, Armoured Knight, Cloncarrig and Pearly Prince. Ordnance came down at the twentieth, Armoured Knight a fence later. Uncle Barney disappeared at the twenty-second, where Witty unseated jockey Slack. Pearly Prince squandered his chance at the twenty-fourth, but veteran Cloncarrig was still in touch, followed far back by Dick Francis on Senlac Hill.

Early Mist was in front followed by Mont Tremblant. For a while the Gold Cup winner looked capable of achieving the double, if not in the same year, but he was conceding 17 lb to the O'Brien-trained eight-year-old and every pound was beginning to hurt. Cloncarrig fell as Irish Lizard, ridden by Bob Turnell, began to improve.

Early Mist thought he had the race won between the last two fences. He lost concentration and began to look around, listening to the Irish welcome. Bryan Marshall had to force him to think about the last, then to realise the danger which Mont Tremblant represented. From that point it was over. Early Mist strode away to win by twenty lengths, finishing so fresh that he had energy to flinch from a newspaper blown on the wind.

Irish Lizard was third, followed by the thirteen-year-old Overshadow, who had been baulked. Senlac Hill was the only other to finish.

The year: 1954
Number of runners: Twenty-nine
Winner: Royal Tan (B. Marshall—11 st 7 lb)
Time: 9 minutes 32⅘ seconds

Royal Tan's victory was well earned. Second to Nickel Coin in 1951, he would have been second to Teal in 1952 if he had survived the last. After that race he was fired and rested while Early Mist became the hero of the O'Brien yard. In 1954 he came back to find himself top weight at 11 st 7 lb, the heavyweights having withdrawn. They included Early Mist, Knock Hard and Mont Tremblant. The way was open for an honest trier and Royal Tan was as honest as they come.

The race began sadly. Whispering Steel, Alberoni, Swinton Hero and Gentle Moya fell at the first. Seconds later Dominick's Bar, ridden by Tim Molony, dropped dead. Minimax and Baire fell at the second; Paris New York at the fourth; Gay Monarch II at the fifth. Legal Joy was killed at the thirteenth, while Statesman, Border Luck and Triple Torch did not get halfway.

Coneyburrow blundered at the water, but Pat Taaffe kept him going. As they approached Becher's for the second time Jack Dowdeswell, a former champion who had never had much luck at Liverpool, had Ordnance well placed behind Irish Lizard, Tudor Line, Royal Tan, Sanperion and Royal Stuart. Ordnance and Prince of Arragon fell at the twenty-third; Royal Stuart refused the twenty-seventh, where poor Coneyburrow broke his neck.

As they approached the second last, three horses had a chance: Tudor Line, ridden by George Slack, O'Brien's second string, Church Town, ridden by T. Taaffe, and Royal Tan, patiently handled by Bryan Marshall. Church Town jumped it first but blundered. Tudor Line led to the last where he jumped towards the right. It had been Royal Tan's bogey fence before and Marshall took no chances. He coaxed the ten-year-old over it, then sat down to ride as good a finish as Aintree has seen in recent years.

For a hundred yards Royal Tan seemed to have it won, but Tudor Line fought back, stealing inches at every stride. Royal Tan answered, and for what seemed a long time, unbearably long, like waiting for a spring to snap, they were giving every ounce, heads straining and forelegs reaching. Royal Tan had the longer neck and got it in front where it mattered most for the narrowest victory since Battleship's.

Irish Lizard, owned by Lord Sefton, was again third. Church Town was fourth. Others to finish were Sanperion, Martinique, Uncle Barney, Southern Coup and Ontray. Punchestown Star broke down at the twenty-eighth.

It was a second successive triumph for the O'Brien-Marshall-Griffin combination; reminiscent of 1918 and 1919 when a combination of trainer, jockey and owner had won twice with Poethlyn.

Bryan Marshall had begun with Atty Persse and had ridden his first winner (on the flat) in 1929 at the age of thirteen. He'd served with Hubert Hartigan and Noel Murless; had ridden jumpers before the war and broken his back; had been commissioned in the 5th Inniskilling Dragoon Guards and wounded in Normandy; had returned to National Hunt racing after the war with age and weight against him. He was thirty years old, weighed 12 st 7 lb and had about twenty winners to his credit. Two seasons later he was champion.

Few knew that three weeks before his victory on Royal Tan he had fractured his jaw in five places when falling at Kempton. Doctors had told him he was 'mad to ride'.

The year: 1955
Number of runners: Thirty
Winner: Quare Times (P. Taaffe—11 st)
Time: 10 minutes 20⅗ seconds

The death of four horses, coming so soon after first-fence calamities and the fiasco of 1951, had revived opposition to the race. Most of the criticisms were ill-directed, however sincere; the wilder accusations of 'barbarity' were echoes of criticisms made more than a hundred years before; yet the opposition was powerful enough to get its views expressed in the House of Lords.

Rain hammered holes in the Liverpool puddles for three days before the race. The going was deep, too deep, it was thought, for newcomer Quare Times, nine years old, owned by Mrs. W. H. Welman, trained by Vincent O'Brien, and ridden by Pat Taaffe. O'Brien, emulating Linde in his serious assault on the

National, had three other runners: Oriental Way, ridden by Fred Winter, Early Mist and Royal Tan. Yet the public preferred another Irish horse, Copp, ridden by Tim Molony, who started 7—1 favourite. Little Yid, disappointing favourite in 1953, was trying again at thirteen years old. Ridden by R. Emery, he was 50—1.

Mariner's Log and Blue Envoy came down at the first, but casualties were mercifully few until the seventh where Copp fell. So did No Response. At the end of the first circuit E.S.B., Dark Stranger, Moogie, Another Rake, Oriental Way, Roman Fire and Munster King II were no longer present.

Sundew was prominent on the second circuit, accompanied by Carey's Cottage, Ontray and Gentle Moya. Irish Lizard, twelve years old and ridden by Scudamore, blundered at Becher's, where Ma's-tu Vu, ridden by Arthur Freeman, began to falter. Little Yid was pulled up. Coming away from Becher's Quare Times was up with Tudor Line, Carey's Cottage and Gigolo.

Tudor Line held the lead until the second last, where Quare Times, revelling in the mud, made rapid progress. Carey's Cottage had nothing left. Gigolo and Gentle Moya could not quicken. It was left to the luckless Tudor Line to chase Quare Times up the gruelling 494 yards from the last fence to the post. He could get no closer than twelve lengths with Carey's Cottage four lengths away third.

Others to finish were Gigolo, Ontray, Gentle Moya, Clearing, Wild Wisdom, Early Mist, Red Rube, Royal Tan, and the bravely consistent Uncle Barney.

O'Brien's third successive win established a formidable record. He had nursed Quare Times for six years, not seriously training him until he was seven, then delaying his National bid until he was nine. Six weeks after winning £8,934 for Mrs. Welman, Quare Times won a hurdle race at Leopardstown. He continued to run although without much success until he was twelve, when he was retired to hunting.

The year: 1956
Number of runners: Twenty-nine
Winner: E.S.B. (D. V. Dick—11 st 3 lb)
Time: 9 minutes 21 seconds

It was the year of Devon Loch, owned by the Queen Mother, ridden by Dick Francis and the unluckiest loser since Limerock in 1917.

King George VI had died in 1952 and his daughter Elizabeth, inheriting the Royal stable, had turned from National Hunt racing to the flat, leaving steeplechasing to her mother who had become respected for her knowledge of breeding and performance as well as liked for her charm. The Queen Mother had won races with Manicou, inherited from Lord Mildmay; her Monaveen had broken a leg at Hurst Park; she'd had some luck with the French-bred Ma's-tu Vu. But Devon Loch was her most serious contender for the biggest steeplechase of the year.

By Devonian out of a mare by Loch Lomond, Devon Loch had been bought in Ireland from Colonel Stephen Hill-Dillon and in his first attempt over fences had given Mont Tremblant a fright at Hurst Park. He developed tendon trouble, was fired, then rested. Trainer Cazalet, whose Fairlawne stable had sent Davy Jones and Cromwell to near-triumph at Aintree, was prepared to wait, sure that this time the luck would turn good.

The Queen Mother came to watch, accompanied by her daughters, by the Princess Royal and by a group of Russian statesmen, including Mr. Malenkov. The March sunshine encouraged a feeling of optimism that this National would see the first Royal victory since 1900.

Vincent O'Brien was represented by Early Mist and Royal Tan, but the morning whisper was for Must, ridden by R. Morrow and backed dramatically from 100—9 to 7—1 favourite. Sundew, ridden by Fred Winter, was second favourite at 8—1, while Ontray, having appeared on the bookmakers' boards at 25—1, shortened rapidly to 100—6.

Must fell at the first. So did Reverend Prince, Early Mist and High Guard. No Response and Mariner's Log fell before

Becher's and Athenian shortly after it. Armorial III, giving Jack Dowdeswell a good ride, made the pace from Sundew, Dunboy II, Witty, and Ma's-tu Vu. Sundew crashed at Becher's on the second circuit, where Royal Tan, Eagle Lodge, Key Royal, E.S.B., Ontray and Devon Loch were prominent. At the Canal Turn Devon Loch was going so strongly that Dick Francis had to steady him.

Gentle Moya blundered. Ontray unseated jockey Curran. Devon Loch was in front at the twenty-eighth and continued to jump brilliantly. He took the last ahead of E.S.B. and Royal Tan, coming away so strongly that it seemed all over bar the shouting.

There was plenty of that. The reception was tumultuous. A Royal victory always gets its cheers, but this din was different. It was genuine. It came from the heart and stung the eyes. It might have startled the horse and shattered his concentration. Years afterwards Dick Francis would remain convinced that Devon Loch flinched from the noise, lost his stride and stumbled and fell. Others would attribute it to hallucination, an attempt to jump a shadow, perhaps to cramp or minor convulsion. Whatever the cause, Devon Loch, fifty yards from the post, with the hats of the crowd already lifted, suddenly dropped, legs spread-eagled, his girths touching the grass. The din was vivid with incredulity and grief.

Seconds before, Dave Dick on E.S.B. had dropped his hands, settling for second place. Now he rode for dear life, getting the ten-year-old home by ten lengths from Gentle Moya and Royal Tan. Others to finish were Eagle Lodge, Key Royal, Martinique, Carey's Cottage, Clearing and Wild Wisdom.

The saddest figure in the history of the race was Dick Francis, walking back to the paddock with the 'winner' who had somehow missed the victory. For trainer Cazalet the disappointment was acute, but the Queen Mother gave no sign as she congratulated Mrs. L. Carver, the owner of the winner.

The year: 1957
Number of runners: Thirty-five
Winner: Sundew (F. T. Winter—11 st 7 lb)
Time: 9 minutes 42⅘ seconds

I remember someone calling 'Fred's won', and suddenly the world was smiling as when justice has been done. Fred Winter was another to come out of the Army without much future, then suddenly to find the luck which makes all things possible. He had his first ride under National Hunt rules on December 26th, 1947, when on leave from the Parachute Regiment. The following day he rode his first winner: Carton in the Kenton handicap 'chase at Kempton. In 1949 he joined Captain Ryan Price's small stable at Lavant and that was the turning point. In his sixth season he became champion with 121 winners. Sundew was his first National winner.

He had ridden the Hudson-trained horse in 1956 and had fallen heavily at Becher's. This time he stuck, surviving mistake after mistake as the eleven-year-old led from the fourth to the end. Fred was sure something must catch him, but Sundew kept pounding as others kept falling and reached the last fence with ears flopping, legs heavy, only his courage intact. He kept 'picking them up and putting them down' while Wyndburgh strained to reach him and Tiberetta battled bravely from the last.

Wyndburgh was second, beaten eight lengths. Tiberetta was third. Others to get round were Glorious Twelfth, Crofter, Goosander, Sydney Jones, E.S.B., Merry Throw, Sandy Jane II, Gentle Moya. China Clipper II, ridden by W. D. Gibson, fell at the last.

Sundew was the only steeplechaser in Frank Hudson's small yard near Henley-in-Arden. His owner, Mrs. G. Kohn, had sent him to the December sales, where he did not reach his reserve of £2,500. Previously she had sold a half-share in E.S.B. before his Aintree win.

The following season Sundew broke his back at Haydock and had to be destroyed.

The year: 1958
Number of runners: Thirty-one
Winner: Mr. What (A. Freeman—10 st)
Time: 10 minutes 1⅕ seconds

The race was worth £13,719 to the winner and the winner was a tough little Irishman, Mr. What; eight years old, trained by T. Taaffe for Mr. D. J. Coughlan, and ridden by Arthur Freeman who had fallen at the first on Rendezvous III the previous year.

Wyndburgh was 6—1 favourite; Hart Royal and Valiant Spark were well supported; while E.S.B. was trying again at the age of twelve.

Rendezvous III, Princess Garter, Valiant Spark, and Longmead were the early fallers. Sentina, ridden by Pat Taaffe, was brought down at Becher's, where Must, the hot tip in 1956 when he had fallen at the first, came down with jockey Morrow. Comedian's Folly ran out and Frozen Credit refused.

Goosander was among the leaders at the water, by which time Ace of Trumps, Glorious Twelfth and Brookling had gone. Approaching Becher's for the second time Mr. What pulled his way to the front, followed by Tiberetta, Green Drill, Wyndburgh and Goosander. Wise Child, Athenian, Hart Royal, Sydney Jones and Pippykin dropped out. Crofter fell at the twentieth.

Mr. What held a commanding lead three out, but took risks with the last, hitting it so heavily that a less accomplished jockey might have been catapulted 'halfway to Walton'. Arthur Freeman, son of huntsman Will Freeman, clung like a leech and Mr. What drew away from Tiberetta to win by twenty lengths. Green Drill was third and Wyndburgh fourth.

Others to finish were Goosander, E.S.B. and Holly Bank. The going was deep, the time of 10 minutes 1⅕ seconds slow. Since Tipperary Tim in 1928 only two others—Caughoo and Quare Times—had won in more than ten minutes.

Mr. What subsequently passed from trainer to trainer, including Peter Cazalet, but in thirty-three attempts he could not win another race.

The year: 1959
Number of runners: Thirty-four
Winner: Oxo (M. Scudamore—10 st 13 lb)
Time: 9 minutes 37⅕ seconds

Two years previously Royston trainer Willie Stephenson had paid 3,000 guineas on behalf of Mr. J. E. Bigg for a big point-to-point horse. Asked what he hoped to do with him, Willie had replied, 'Win a National,' and in 1959 he judged the eight-year-old ready. Michael Scudamore, a farmer's son and another product of point-to-pointing, was engaged to ride and the Royston stable needed only luck.

It had luck in plenty, for only accident prevented the persistent Wyndburgh, the MacMoffat of his day, from winning at last. As he jumped Becher's for the second time, a stirrup iron snapped. Tim Brookshaw, in his championship season, recovered quickly and slipped the other foot free, riding without stirrups and calling to Scudamore on Oxo, 'Look—no feet.' It should have been the end of Wyndburgh's chances, but Brookshaw never gave in easily. He rode a memorable race, keeping Wyndburgh in touch until Valentine's, then forcing the nine-year-old in pursuit of Oxo between the last two fences.

Oxo hit the last, yet stood up. He came away with a long lead, but Wyndburgh whittled it stride by stride, getting to within two lengths and clinging, never able to quicken yet never yielding. It was a triumph of horse and rider over adversity, worthy of a place in Aintree folklore.

Mr. What was third, despite casting a plate halfway. Tiberetta, another of the Carsey mould, was the only other to finish. Unluckiest of the fallen was the mare, Kerstin, brought down at Becher's when among the leaders on the second circuit. Other jockeys brought back their hard-luck stories, including J. Hudson who had made some of the running on Turmoil only to be baulked at the Canal Turn; where Cannobie Lee, ridden by

David Nicholson, had been similarly impeded.

That only four of thirty-four got round struck a match to new controversy. Changes were demanded in the weights, the construction of the fences, reviving arguments almost a hundred years old. The controversy, rising at times to hysteria, brought a troubled decade to a troubled end. Another was about to begin which would make the National a European as well as a nation-wide event; which would see Russian horses competing for the first time; and during which the future of Aintree as a racecourse would be discussed in newspapers, weighing-rooms, pubs and kitchens and finally the House of Lords.

15

Steeplechasing was first televised on January 24th, 1948, when the B.B.C. took cameras to Sandown Park. They relayed two steeplechases and a hurdle race, and the response was immediate. Viewers discovered what the people of Liverpool had found 110 years before; that steeplechasing is a spectacle more exciting and rewarding than the flat, alight with perils and valour, compelling involvement without need to bet and so fraught with surprises that no horse is a 'certainty'.

The B.B.C. understood the possibilities, but the development of its service was slow. Not until the late 1950s was the medium available to all parts of Britain and by then commercial television had established itself. Where there had been famine there was glut. In Wales, Scotland and the extreme tip of Cornwall, viewers had either B.B.C. or I.T.V. or both. On either channel steeplechasing was a top attraction.

Televising the Grand National presented special problems, but in 1960 the B.B.C. overcame them for the first time. The race was a 'natural', commanding an estimated audience of ten million, excluding the millions in other countries who watched through the Eurovision link. If the ghost of William Lynn was around he must have been fascinated and delighted, for what he had visualised as a national event, appealing to people from all walks of life, had become international in a way beyond his wildest dreams.

The first commentators were Peter O'Sullevan, Clive Graham and Peter Bromley, an accomplished team, bringing to racing a professionalism which the B.B.C. does not always show to other sports. Peter Montague Evans and Derek Hart also took part, and the producers were Ray Lakeland, Dennis Monger and John Vernon. At the turn of a switch the race was there, in a corner of the living-room, sitting-room, lounge, front-room, viewing-room; call it what you will. Suddenly newspaper names were faces; legendary fences were real; horses who had been only names on the sports pages, waiting for the family pin to decide what Mother would back this year, became alive and tired and brave and frightened.

The largest audience for any steeplechase in the world watched the preliminaries for the 1960 race half-fearful that it would be another fiasco, another 'massacre'; that something terrible would happen and that it would hurt the more because suddenly they were 'there'. Or almost 'there'. Perhaps better than 'there', for those who were at Aintree saw much of the race only from a distance, missing the detail, the expressions, the sounds of the spruce as horses brushed through. Sounds like the sea, as alive and as menacing; sounds which you couldn't hear if you were there and cold and tiptoeing.

So suddenly it was different. After 123 years those who were there ceased to be privileged. The privileged were at home, at armchair ease, with their shoes off and their braces showing, seeing more for nothing than the bowlers and county tweeds could see for folding money. It was a kind of revolution in its way. No wonder television was mistrusted.

The year: 1960
Number of runners: Twenty-six
Winner: Merryman II (G. Scott—10 st 12 lb)
Time: 9 minutes 26⅕ seconds

Lord Sefton, senior steward at Aintree, warned jockeys and riders to go a sensible gallop in the early stages and to avoid bunching near the rails. The words were timely; the result was a spectacle mercifully free of serious accident, enabling an audience throughout Europe to see steeplechasing at its best. You could be proud of the National that year. You could say without irony or bitterness that no other nation had a race like it. You could even inflate a bit and boast that no other nation ever would. The best thing about it was the result. The best horse won.

Only Lotoray fell at the first. Knoxtown and Wyndburgh went at Becher's, although you felt that by now old Wyndburgh should have known better. Andy Scot fell at the Canal Turn and Jonjo at Valentine's. Any fall must be serious to somebody, but compared with the shambles of the early 1950s, the falls seemed like death in an old-fashioned Western. They hurt no one.

Turning towards the country for the second time Merryman II, fencing boldly in the fashion of a hunter who had served his apprenticeship in hunter 'chases, went to the front with Badanloch, Clear Profit, Tea Fiend, Sabaria and Green Drill. Team Spirit disappeared at Becher's, where Cannobie Lee refused. Aliform and Pendle Lady fell.

You could hear the Northern counties cheering as Merryman came to the last in front, then stayed on with a generosity as big as his courage to win by fifteen lengths. Badanloch was second, ridden by Stan Mellor. Clear Profit was third and Tea Fiend fourth. Sabaria, Green Drill and Arles got round.

It was a third National victory for trainer Crump; a first for jockey Gerry Scott; and a first for Miss W. Wallace, who became the first unmarried woman to own the winner.

The year: 1961
Number of runners: Thirty-five
Winner: Nicolaus Silver (*H. Beasley—10 st 11 lb*)
Time: 9 minutes 22⅔ seconds

The prize money jumped from £13,134 in 1960 to £20,020; an astonishing figure in a sport which still had steeplechases worth less than £200 to the winner. Part was contributed by the organisers; part by the Irish Hospitals Sweepstake, which had been contributing since 1958; for the first time a commercial company added £5,000. The company was Messrs. Schweppes, a generous sponsor of National Hunt races.

The fences were altered, partly in deference to criticism, chiefly in the hope of attracting top-class steeplechasers to Aintree. Wing-Commander Peter Vaux, senior National Hunt steward, supervised a change of shape. Hitherto the fences had been upright. Now they were sloped on the take-off side, giving a horse another yard in which to see the fence and to time his take-off. Many falls had been caused less by inability to jump than by horses getting too close.

A further change was the lowering of the top weight to 12 st. These measures, the increase of prize money, the alteration of fences and reduction of top weight, had one urgent purpose; to persuade owners and trainers that good horses could be fairly risked at Aintree. They were being asked to forget Prince Regent, doomed by top weight and 'dying' under it.

Immediate top weights were the Russian horses, Reljef and Grifel, trained on a snow-covered trotting track in Moscow and ridden by B. Ponomarenko and V. Prakhov. They were compelled to give weight to three previous winners; 2 lb to Merryman II, 5 lb to Mr. What, 6 lb to Oxo. Their riders' only experience of long-distance steeplechasing was a gruelling cross-country event in Czechoslovakia, similar to early steeplechases in Britain in that falls are frequent and the fallen rider can often get back to win.

Jonjo, ridden by Pat Taaffe, was 7—1 favourite. Derek Ancil rode Merryman in the absence of Gerry Scott through injury. Hunters Breeze, O'Malley Point and Scottish Flight were well backed, while Nicolaus Silver, trained by Fred Rimell and ridden by Bobby Beasley, might have been shorter than 28—1 if there hadn't developed a prejudice against grey horses, as there used to be a prejudice against black or pale chestnut.

April Queen, Floater and Clover Cud fell at the first. Brian Oge, Kingstel, Carrasco and Taxidermist were soon gone, followed by Wily Oriental and Jimuru. The first Russian went at

Valentine's, where Ponomarenko was unseated. Grifel had also fallen but Prakhov remounted to complete the circuit. He pulled up at the water.

Fresh Winds, trained by W. H. Whiston and ridden by Roy Edwards, led into the country and continued in front until the nineteenth, where he came down. Vivant, Tea Fiend and Bantry Bay had already gone. Double Crest refused at Becher's, where Scudamore pulled up Oxo.

Merryman, Wyndburgh and Kilmore were among the leaders as they approached Valentine's. Nicolaus Silver began to improve and two fences out was in front, closely followed by Merryman and O'Malley Point. He jumped the last with stylish dash, then held on by five lengths to win from Merryman. O'Malley Point, ridden by Paddy Farrell, was a neck away third.

Others to finish were Scottish Flight, Kilmore, Wyndburgh, Jonjo, Badanloch, Team Spirit, Siracusa, Mr. What, Ernest, Sabaria and Irish Coffee.

Trainer Rimell had won with E.S.B. in 1956, but it was a first National win for Bobby Beasley; the grandson of Harry who had won on Come Away in 1891. His wife is the daughter of Arthur Thompson.

There was no long rest for Nicolaus Silver. Having won £20,000 for his owner, Mr. C. Vaughan, he ran in the Whitbread Gold Cup, finishing an honourable second to Pas Seul. His success did something to ridicule the prejudice against greys. In the words of an old horseman, 'Any colour's right if they're good enough.'

The year: 1962
Number of runners: Thirty-two
Winner: Kilmore (F. Winter—10 st 4 lb)
Time: 9 minutes 50 seconds

Fred Winter's second National victory gave him special pleasure; not because Kilmore was a favourite horse, but because the twelve-year-old was trained by Captain Ryan Price. The link between jockey and trainer could be traced to 1949 when Captain Price had had a small stable at Lavant and Fred had been looking for winners. They had come together, each supplying the other's need, and that F. T. Winter should ride the first National winner to be trained by R. Price seemed an apt climax to long friendship.

The weather helped. In spring-like weather and on good ground there were plenty in the field who would surely have run Kilmore out of it during the final mile. But heavy rain had churned the going to mud. Light-weights were favoured, especially reliable jumpers who could be trusted to try every yard. Kilmore had the qualifications. So had Mr. What and Wyndburgh. All were twelve years old, and all were to show their juniors how to get round Aintree in the mud.

Well-fancied Springbok, ridden by Pat Buckley, fell at the first, but mishaps were few until the water, where Dandy Tim crashed when disputing the lead. Fred Winter was riding a George Stevens type of race; keeping Kilmore out of trouble, hoarding every yard, waiting for younger horses to knock each other out.

The bold Frenchman's Cove, 7—1 favourite and ridden by Stan Mellor, threatened to take them off their legs until the nineteenth, where he was brought down by Duplicator and Team Spirit. This was the turning point. The class horse was gone. The way was open for the old dependables.

Kilmore did not show until the Canal Turn, where Gay Navarree and Fredith's Son were prominent. After that he made steady progress, stealing through the tired and toiling without seeming to be a serious threat. He jumped the second last ahead of Gay Navarree and in a triumph of jockeyship, as deceptive as a conjuring trick, took the lead before the last. Not until then did the stands realise that Kilmore was about to win. They rose to him, or perhaps to his jockey, as he jumped the last with no more fuss than he had jumped the rest, then galloped on, calling up the strength which patient riding had conserved.

Dark Venetian, ridden by Paddy Cowley, made up ground

and threatened to grab a place; but Wyndburgh and Mr. What were elder statesmen of the Liverpool game, too wise to be cheated at this stage. They held on to take second and third places, each in his own solemn time, never near enough to frighten the winner.

Others to finish were Gay Navarree, Fredith's Son, Dark Venetian, Nicolaus Silver, Cannobie Lee, Ernest, Clover Bud, Blonde Warrior, Solfen, Merryman II, Colledge Master, Fortron, Politics and Clear Profit.

It was the end of a long and honourable road for Wyndburgh. He was the pet of his owner, Miss R. P. Wilkinson, and she decided that having achieved his hat-trick of seconds, the old gentleman had done enough.

The year: 1963
Number of runners: Forty-seven
Winner: Ayala (P. Buckley—10 st)
Time: 9 minutes 35⅘ seconds

The climax of this race was another confrontation between amateur and professional. It had happened before and the amateur had sometimes won; Lord Manners on Seaman in 1882, Douglas Campbell on The Soarer in 1896, Captain Petre on Lovely Cottage in 1946. The list is honourable and the name of John Lawrence was almost added to it.

He rode Carrickbeg, a seven-year-old, owned by another amateur, Gay Kindersley. At the last the partnership of promising steeplechaser and amateur rider seemed to have the race won; but when horse and rider are over the last at Aintree, both have a lot still to do. Carrickbeg promised to do it.

At the 'elbow', where horses bear left towards the finish, he was still on his own, apparently as certain to win as Devon Loch had seemed in 1956. But what had happened to Dick Francis and the Queen Mother's horse had taught the stands not to cheer too soon. They held back their cheers in a dreadful moment of doubt, then set free a roar of warning. A challenger was coming. They might not have been sure of his name, for the name of Ayala was lost among the bottom weights on the race-card; but Ayala he was, coming like a train and ridden by Pat Buckley, who was acquiring a formidable reputation in the North.

Lawrence sensed the danger and tried to fight back, but Carrick was exhausted, too. You could see their weariness, feel their desperation. A hundred yards out the crowd thought the amateur still might do what none had done since Captain Petre. But Buckley had a Northern toughness, a professional determination. He out-rode the amateur to get Ayala level fifty yards from the post. Twenty strides later Ayala was in front and the winning margin proved longer than it seemed; three-quarters of a length. Hawa's Song was third and Team Spirit fourth.

Springbok, made 10—1 favourite despite his fall at the first in 1962, ran well until two out. Kilmore, thirteen years old and again ridden by Fred Winter, got round but venerable Mr. What was brought down at the twenty-seventh. For twenty-five fences Out And About, dashingly ridden by Josh Gifford, threatened to be a runaway winner.

Those who stood up were Springbok, Kilmore, Owen's Sedge, French Lawyer, Dark Venetian, Nicolaus Silver, Eternal, Chavara, Carraroe, Siracusa, Sham Fight, Blonde Warrior, Loyal Tan, Woodbrown, O'Malley Point, Forty Secrets, Dandy Tim and the disappointing Frenchman's Cove, who was never seen with a chance.

Those who failed to get round were Mr. Jones, Mr. What, Out And About, Good Gracious, Jonjo, Peacetown, Gay Navarree, Wingless, Avenue Neuilly, Vivant, Connie II, Wartown, Look Happy, Merganser, Magic Tricks, Solonace, Loving Record, Dagmar Gittell, Moyrath, Seas End, College Don, Reprieved, Holm Star, Capricorn and Melilla.

Ayala, owned by hairdresser Mr. P. B. Raymond and trained by Keith Piggott, father of Lester and son of Ernest, subsequently ran nine times without winning. On seven occasions he did not even get round.

The year: 1964
Number of runners: Thirty-three
Winner: Team Spirit (G. W. Robinson—10 st 3 lb)
Time: 9 minutes 47 seconds

Purple Silk (J. Keneally), Out And About (B. Gregory) and Peacetown (R. Edwards) were the spectacular front runners, racing like fly-weights fight; all action, intent on knocking each other out. At one stage they threatened to get away with it, but there's still much to be said for George Stevens' early caution; for, in Fred Winter's words, 'hunting round the first time' until the race has settled down.

Out And About was the first to weaken, but Peacetown lasted until Valentine's, where he jumped like a tired fly-weight throwing his last punch. Purple Silk was still there at the last. It was then that Team Spirit, twelve years old and running in his fifth National, came strongly, superbly ridden by Willie Robinson who was to share the rise and fall of Mill House.

In other years Team Spirit had jumped safely but slowly, seeming to lack the attack which every winner needs; but Robinson had remained convinced that—like Frigate and Why Not more than fifty years before—he would find reward some time. There was genuine affection in the cheering as old Team Spirit forged ahead of Purple Silk and held on by less than a length. Peacetown was third. Eternal, ridden by young Stephen Davenport who would soon turn professional, made up ground from Valentine's to finish fourth.

Again there was support for Springbok; again he disappointed. Gerry Scott had him second at Valentine's, but from three out he weakened quickly, seeming to lack resolution. Others to finish were Pontin-Go, April Rose, Baxier, Crobeg, Pappageno's Cottage, John O' Groats, Supersweet, Claymore, Out And About and Sea Knight.

Among the fallen were Flying Wild, who came down with David Mould at the first; and the Queen Mother's Laffy, who fell with Bill Rees at the fourth. The 1963 winner, Ayala, went at the fifteenth, while Pas Seul, winner of the Cheltenham Gold

Cup in 1960 but years passed his best, came down at the twelfth.

Others who did not get round were Border Flight, Lizawake, Centre Circle, Time, Reproduction, Merganser, Gale Force X, Groomsman, L'Empereur, Red Thorn, Reprieved, Beau Normand, Dancing Rain and Kilmore, giving Fred Winter his last ride in a National.

It was Fulke Walwyn's first National success as a trainer, although he had won on Reynoldstown in 1937. For the first time the ownership was credited to three people; Messrs. J. K. Goodman, Gamble North, and R. B. Woodard. They were Americans and their success gave New York something to cheer for the first time since Battleship in 1938. Their prize was £20,280, but this was the last year Messrs. Schweppes contributed.

It was also the year in which the owners of Aintree declared that the racecourse was no longer a viable proposition. Land acquired from Lord Sefton in 1949 and supposedly protected by a covenant, had a greater value as a site for houses or factories. Such a use would supply a growing need, for the city was expanding. Liverpool could not live without land and although the sentimental might consider Aintree hallowed, the claim that so many acres could be put to fuller and more productive use seemed spurious only to those who placed tradition before the needs of a community or racing before anything.

Mrs. M. Topham declared an intention to sell to Capital and Counties Ltd., and the racing world heard the news with a queer ambivalence. For years owners and trainers had realised that Aintree was declining as the traditional home of steeplechasing. In public sometimes and in private often they had been critical, even despairing; giving their support to other meetings, helping to promote Cheltenham to a stature which rivalled Aintree. Yet they sought to defend it from summary change, just as those who never pass within a cathedral or contribute to its maintenance might rush to defend it from demolition.

The desire to sell was promptly contested and the processes of law served to block any immediate change. Plans for the Grand National of 1965 continued while rumours persisted that it would be the last. One result of such threat was the stimulation of attendance. Thousands left their television sets and returned to Aintree, giving financial support through the turnstiles as they had not done since the early 1950s. This might have been no more significant than the rush to travel on a branch-line train when it makes its last journey, but it expressed an awareness that even those events which are rooted in deep traditions cannot prosper without active support.

The rejuvenated crowds were to see one of the finest finishes in the history of the race; the defeat of a horse who won affection in failure similar to that accorded Prince Regent; and the achievement of an American ambition nearly fifty years old.

The year: 1965
Number of runners: Forty-seven
Winner: Jay Trump (Mr. C. Smith—11 st 5 lb)
Time: 9 minutes 30⅗ seconds

This was it; an 'All-American' victory, achieved by a horse American-bred, American-owned and American-ridden. This was three times better than Rubio in 1908, who had been American-bred. Or Sergeant Murphy and Jack Horner, where the American involvement had been ownership only. It was even better than Battleship, who had been American-bred and American-owned, but who had been ridden by a Briton. 'Tommy' Smith was the first American to ride an American-bred and American-owned winner, and it's a wonder they didn't make him President.

The victory wasn't lightly achieved. Owner Mrs. M. Stephenson sent Jay Trump to Fred Winter's yard at Uplands in plenty of time to become acclimatised and to qualify. Tommy Smith came, too; totally inexperienced over English fences, in need of a tuition as patient as Ben Land had given in the nineteenth century. In his preliminary races Smith didn't impress the experts; but the experts are wrong so often that their small regard was almost a commendation. Tommy Smith, his lessons carefully and humbly learned, was to succeed where all the amateurs since Captain Petre had failed.

Jay Trump was one half of the thrilling finish. The other half was Freddie, a former hunter-'chaser, bred in Ireland and trained in Scotland by his owner, Mr. R. Tweedie, who had ridden Venturesome Knight in the National of 1940.

Aintree loved Freddie from the start, installing him 7—2 favourite, the shortest price since Golden Miller in 1935. It was an astonishing tribute to a newcomer; since it has been estimated that the chances of any horse even getting round are less than 3—1. Ridden by Pat McCarron and carrying 11 st 10 lb, as well as half the money in Scotland, the dark eight-year-old went out for the greatest race of his life. The full story is told in *A Horse Called Freddie*, including the personal involvement of the Tweedie family, akin to the dedicated amateurism behind Sunloch's victory in 1914. There is not space here to repeat it, only to stress that if this Grand National had been the last at Aintree there could have been no finer curtain.

Ayala, the winner in 1963, fell at the first with Stan Mellor, but the rest of the field kept out of trouble until Ronald's Boy fell at the third, giving Gay Kindersley, the owner of Carrickbeg, another unlucky National. Red Tide fell at the fourth and you could hear the sounds of tumbling money, for he'd been backed from 40—1 to 33—1. Nedsmar went at the sixth. So did Ruby Glen, Forgotten Dreams, Barleycroft, Sizzle-On and Crobeg. Phebu and Peacetown were among the leaders until Phebu fell, brought down by the riderless Red Tide. At the water Freddie and Jay Trump were in the leading group, accompanied by Peacetown, Rondetto, Kapeno and The Rip.

As they approached Becher's for the second time Loving Record, Rainbow Battle and Vultrix began to show. So did L'Empereur, ridden by Mr. J. Ciechanowski, who had inherited the determination of nineteenth-century amateurs to win a National. Mr. Chris Collins, soon to become the top amateur, was close with Mr. Jones. The pace quickened as Tommy Smith on Jay Trump began to make his move. You could imagine him trying to think like Fred Winter, even to become Fred Winter.

Rondetto fell at the twenty-sixth and Peacetown faded. Suddenly Freddie was in front, earlier perhaps than McCarron would have wished. Freddie began the long run home, his tongue lolling and head low, his thin blaze as livid as a scar. He was followed by Vultrix, Rainbow Battle, The Rip, Loving Record and with ominous quiet by Jay Trump.

Two out there were only two in it. Jay Trump passed Freddie before the last and jumped it in front, gaining the inches which were to matter. Again talented amateur and top-class professional were locked in long struggle. This time the amateur won. Jay Trump held off 'the darling of all Scotland' to win by three-quarters of a length. Chris Collins was third on Mr. Jones, twenty lengths away. Rainbow Battle was fourth.

Others who finished were The Rip, Loving Record, Tant Pis, Brown Diamond, April Rose, Culleenhouse, Peacetown and Moyrath.

Those who did not get round were Rondetto, Kapeno, Ayala, Time, Dark Venetian, Red Tide, Pontin-Go, Leedsy, Ronald's Boy, Bold Biri, Groomsman, Blonde Warrior, Nedsmar, Forgotten Dreams, Black Spot, Lizawake, Reproduction, Sword Flash, Vulcano, Quintin Bay, Cutlette, Mr. McTaffy, Barleycroft, Ruby Glen, Crobeg, Solonace, Phebu, Sizzle-On, French Cottage, Coleen Star, Ballygowan, Fearless Cavalier and Leslie.

The prize of £22,041 included a contribution of £10,000 by the recently constituted Betting Levy Board. The Betting, Gaming and Lotteries Act of 1963 had for the first time and to the material benefit of the sport, brought bookmakers' profits within the tax net.

Freddie went back to Scotland and became a national hero. Jay Trump ultimately returned to America. For Fred Winter, recently retired from riding and in his first season as a trainer, it was a triumph of coaching as well as of training.

The year: 1966
Number of runners: Forty-seven
Winner: Anglo (T. Norman—10 st)
Time: 9 minutes 52⅘ seconds

The legal battle over the future of Aintree had passed through the courts to the House of Lords, where their lordships, reversing previous decisions, had ruled that the covenant was not binding. For this reason the National of 1966 seemed likely to be the last, the National Hunt Committee having made it clear that its members would not favour a pale substitute held on any other course.

Freddie was an even shorter favourite, backed on the day from 11—2 to 11—4. The bagpipes were there again, waiting to play him into the winner's enclosure and simultaneously into history; for no one in Sir Walter Scott country would concede the possibility of further failure. His rivals promised to be Forest Prince, The Fossa, Highland Wedding, Kapeno, Popham Down and the stylish What A Myth, trained to the minute by Ryan Price but prone to risk a fence.

Few noticed Anglo, the second National contender to be trained by Fred Winter. The eight-year-old chestnut had done little after beginning his racing career as Flag of Convenience. Bred by Mr. W. Kennedy, of Downpatrick, a failure on the flat and bought by Mr. J. Nichols, a Huntingdon farmer, for 110 guineas, Anglo was bottom of the handicap and 50—1. He seemed to have no more chance than Fujino-O, the Japanese entry, ridden by J. King.

For the first time in years a big field jumped the first without mishap. The first faller was Rough Tweed, heavily backed from 33—1 to 22—1. He came down at the third and again you could hear the North Country wincing in its pocket. Packed Home, Popham Down, and Groomsman were soon missing and the field was spreadeagled as Forest Prince, Quintin Bay, Highland Wedding, Gale Force X and Freddie led them over the water.

The second circuit took quick toll as horses tired in the mud. Irish Day, Game Purston, Pontin-Go, Black Spot and

Monarch's Thought dropped out. Harry Black was prominent at the nineteenth, where Major Hitch and Scottish Final fell. Greek Scholar fell at the twenty-second. Meanwhile Freddie was pounding sternly towards what promised to be Scotland's first success in a National. They know how to cheer in Scotland and they had cheers in their throats as Freddie chased Forest Prince towards Valentine's. Behind him were The Fossa, Highland Wedding, Quintin Bay and Anglo. Gale Force X had blown himself out, while Flying Wild was plainly beaten and What A Myth had fallen.

Scotland could be forgiven for supposing that Freddie had only to take Forest Prince to be sure of victory. But Anglo proved the faster, snatching the lead at the second last. Freddie went after him with the dour persistence of a genuine stayer, but he was conceding 21 lb and each pound began to count double, treble, as they reached the last. Anglo jumped it as well as he had jumped the first and drew away despite all that Scotland could do to restrain him. Freddie never gave up. His tongue wagging in that grotesque way which had become his trademark, he fought every stride, but a hundred yards out it ceased to be a race.

Anglo drew away to win by twenty lengths. Forest Prince was five lengths away third. The Fossa, giving Terry Biddlecombe his best National so far, was fourth, followed by Mr. Nick Gasalee on Jim's Tavern. Others who finished were Quintin Bay, Norther, Highland Wedding, Vulcano, Gale Force X, Big George and Loving Record.

Those who did not finish were What A Myth, Rough Tweed, Kapeno, Packed Home, Greek Scholar, Brown Diamond, Popham Down, Pontin-Go, Game Purston, Supersweet, Major Hitch, Irish Day, Scottish Final, Flame Cap, Black Spot, Harry Black, Flying Wild, Stirling, Vultrix, Solimyth, Bold Biri, April Rose, L'Empereur, Willow King, Royal Ruse, Mac's Flare, In Haste, My Gift, Fujino-O, Monarch's Thought, Groomsman, Valouis, Leslie and Dorimont. There was also King Pin, ridden by Mr. Tim Durant, a venerable American who had backed himself to get round. He pulled up at the twentieth.

Anglo was ridden by Tim Norman, a West Country jockey who had competed in gymkhanas as a schoolboy. Fred Winter became the first trainer since Vincent O'Brien to prepare the winner in successive years, and the first in the history of the race to do it within two years of retiring from the saddle.

Owned by Mr. S. Levy, who had paid 2,500 guineas for him, Anglo was only eight years old, yet like other National winners, including Ayala, Russian Hero and E.S.B., he never showed such form again.

The year: 1967
Number of runners: Forty-four
The winner: Foinavon (J. Buckingham—10 st)
Time: 9 minutes 49⅗ seconds

A great race is high drama, but high drama is never far from farce. When Hamlet's trousers fall down nothing can save the play, and the trousers of this drama fell suddenly at the twenty-third fence.

Until then the star actors were performing creditably, promising to do all that the morning papers had predicted. Nick Gasalee had persuaded Kapeno over Becher's for the second time, which was more than Dave Dick or David Mould had been able to do in previous years. Josh Gifford thought he would win on the hot favourite Honey End, while Brian Fletcher shared that confidence on Red Alligator. Pat McCarron was sure it would prove third time lucky for Freddie. Suddenly the ludicrous happened.

Riderless Popham Down prepared to jump the twenty-third as he had jumped the rest. Abruptly he changed his mind and darted along the fence, colliding with Rutherfords, bringing down Limeking and Different Class, all of them baulking twenty others in a confusion reminiscent of the Canal Turn in 1928. Of course it was not the end of the race, any more than an accident to Hamlet is the end of the play. While the stars and featured players were sorting themselves out, one of the small type leaped into the limelight, like the Second Grave-Digger taking over while Hamlet gets his trousers up. It couldn't happen, yet it did. The crowds didn't believe it even as they watched.

The 'Second Grave-Digger' was Foinavon. Someone recognised the blinkers, the tartan cap. Someone shouted his name as in 1928 someone had shouted, with similar incredulity, 'Tipperary Tim'. The incredulity of the stands was shared by a man watching television in his Finchampstead home. He was Mr. C. Watkins, the owner, who had not bothered to attend. Neither had trainer John Kempton, standing incredulous before a television screen at Worcester after riding in a hurdle race. They watched in fascinated disbelief as their derided entry, who had not won in two seasons, galloped off with the play.

Meanwhile the featured players were sorting themselves out. Josh Gifford turned Honey End for another run. Terry Biddlecombe on Greek Scholar followed him. David Mould tried to catch Different Class. Paddy Broderick caught Kirtle Lad. Brian Fletcher, a young Northern jockey with a bright future, remounted Red Alligator. Princeful, Castle Falls, Rondetto and What A Myth were in the confusion. Pat McCarron tried four times to get Freddie over.

Jockey John Buckingham, engaged for the ride only three days before, glanced back once, then kept Foinavon going; like the Second Grave-Digger determined to say everyone's lines before retribution catches up. Honey End, furiously ridden by Gifford, was the nearest of those who threatened retribution. Red Alligator and Greek Scholar were little behind. The stands didn't know whether to laugh or cry or to cheer the farce while it lasted. The bookmakers had no doubts. They were cheering in expectation of a 'skinner'.

Foinavon won by fifteen lengths in a time faster than those recorded by Anglo, Kilmore, Mr. What and Sundew among recent winners. Honey End was second, Red Alligator third and Greek Scholar fourth.

Others who finished were Packed Home, Solbina, Aussie, Scottish Final, What A Myth, Kapeno, Quintin Bay, Bob-A-

Job, Steel Bridge, Castle Falls, Ross Sea, Rutherfords, Freddie and Game Purston.

Those who did not get round were Kilburn, Bassnet, Dorimont, April Rose, Ronald's Boy, Aerial III, Tower Road, Border Fury, Meon Valley, Lucky Domino, Anglo, Forecastle, The Fossa, Norther, Dun Widdy, Penvulgo, Harry Black, Vulcano, Leedsy, Princeful, Limeking, Different Class, Rondetto, Barberyn and Kirtle Lad. The other to fall was Popham Down, who tumbled at the first with Macer Gifford, then struggled up and continued riderless, jumping every fence without hesitation until the fateful twenty-third.

The Tote paid odds of 445—1 compared with the official starting price of 100—1. Foinavon went back to his stable at Compton, Berkshire, faintly embarrassed by his daring like the Second Grave-Digger who finds himself to be Hamlet after all. It was the end for Freddie. Within six months he developed heart trouble and was retired.

16

The jockeys are yawning and that's a sign. They are amused by poor jokes and that's another. They have weighed out for the National of 1968 and have nothing to do except wait and make sure about their St. Christopher medallions; to fold their arms and pluck their cuff-bands and fret their whips against their boots. The yawns are always biggest before the biggest race.

In this tension any joke is better than none and the best joke is a telegram from jockey Johnny Gamble: 'Sorry can't be there —if there are any spare rides, let David Coleman have them.' David Coleman, one of the ablest of television commentators, would enjoy that one.

Time for a smoke, dragging down the fumes. Time to kid American amateur Tim Durant about being a grandfather, especially in Hollywood where all the girls are supposed to look like film stars. Time for small talk about tonight, tomorrow, about where they'll be riding next week, because there mustn't be time to think.

The jockeys listen to the sounds outside like actors listening to an audience before the curtain goes up. Soon they'll be called out, but none will want to be first. They'll gather near the doorway, shy and vulnerable, not yet promoted above ordinary men, waiting for somebody to be first.

There is sunshine in the paddock and that's an omen. Hearts

respond to it like birds; flowers respond by nodding their colours. The flowers in the centre of the paddock are red tulips and white hyacinths. Owners have sprigs of white heather on their lapels. Owners' wives and daughters have lucky charms chiming on their wrists. People crowd the green bank beside the trees, looking down on the slow parade; admiring the sun in the cosseted shines as forty-five horses walk politely, with only an occasional toss of head or fret of tail. Their feet make prints on the red sand path.

It's a democratic crowd, for the National has been always a democratic race. Mothers clutch big handbags and talk broad Lancashire, reminding us of Gracie Fields when love was on the dole and Sally in the alley; elegant men in tailored tweeds; pretty girls in hats of straw, bought for National day, red because it's the fashionable colour and all with long ribbons like grannie; formidable women in hats of green felt, their voices loud and excited, the sort which lost us an Empire; Irishmen with hunting horns and bugles; and old-time jockeys, smiling deep lines into their faces and remembering Reynoldstown.

Film stars Burgess Meredith and Gregory Peck are supposed to be here and that's a tip. Gregory Peck has come to see his horse Different Class, 17—2 favourite and ridden by David Mould. But there's a more furtive whisper for Red Alligator, owned by Mr. John Manners, a Bishop Auckland butcher and trained in the North by Denys Smith. His jockey is twenty-year-old Brian Fletcher, who rode him into third place last year when Foinavon was villain or comedian or perhaps just opportunist.

We can get 100—7 against Red Alligator. The man next to us has risked it and is beginning to worry, because if he goes home 'skint' and the missus finds out the rest of the week-end will be murder. He worries more when an anonymous voice confides that Great Lark is the one. The voice is Irish and Great Lark is as Irish as 'Good morning, Father', and what a lark it will be on the mail-boat if Tommy Carberry brings the brown mare in.

Jockeys come to the ring, and the sun finds new colours to rejoice in. Daffodils beneath the number board get excited by so much competition. They wag a golden song and clamour to be noticed. The jockeys join trainers and owners and owners' wives and daughters in forty-five groups; each a little huddle of smiles and nods and keeping fingers crossed. A bell rings; attendants turn their horses inwards as obediently and precisely as soldiers; trainers take off paddock sheets and tighten girths; jockeys hold back a boot for boosting. Suddenly they are up and promoted, taller than ordinary men, looking down on the faces looking up. Now the faces looking up are anxious because something might happen, something incredible like last year, something terrible like death.

There are minutes of fiddle with stirrups and leathers and chin-straps and reins. Jockeys tie their knots, mindful of Lord Mildmay and Davy Jones in far-off 1936. Horses come from the ring and walk around, shuffling into numerical order. Foinavon is twentieth, his blinkers big and shining, like schoolboy conkers. They pass before the stands and suddenly the stands are full, stuffed by late-comers who hurry from Tote and bookmakers' boards, squeezing into inches and tiptoeing, panting their private little prayers. The Irish wave to Tommy Carberry and the jockey looks up and answers.

The stands cast a shadow on the grass but the horses keep away from it like cats from water. They pass down a lane of sunshine, their feet lilting in private melodies like singing in your bath. At the end of the parade the attendants slip the leading tapes; white tapes in honour of the day, like blanco-parades in the Army. Jockeys take over. The horses turn and flounce and begin to canter, feeling the ground and testing it, suspicious of mud and finding none, then trying to stretch in celebration. They pass beneath the starting gate to the first fence and spend a minute in serious contemplation. Jockeys talk among themselves as they jog back to the gate which isn't a gate, only a tape, sagging across the green and flopping against the horses' chests. There is more anxious fiddling with girths and leathers. The bowler hat is the starter. He climbs to what a classic cliché calls his rostrum. There's a long wait which isn't long according to ordinary time. There's a rising tension, a shuffling for places.

Grandfather Durant, sixty-eight years old and probably the oldest since William Lynn first had the idea, takes no chances. He's on the outside with Highlandie, conceding the inside to professionals who will show no charity to a grey amateur. Tim Durant knows he cannot win, although John Buckingham knew that last year and what happened then? But he's determined to get round and has taken 5—1 against that; investing £100 and accepting the promise of a case of champagne from sporting bookmakers who like their amateurs to be different.

The tape lurches up and they're away, running from us like colours in a dream. Jockeys prepare for the first and in any steeplechase the first fence is never easy. Ford Ord blunders. Poor Tim Norman, who had his triumph on Anglo in 1966, plunges with arms out like a diver. The Fossa leads Valbus, Quintin Bay and Princeful towards Becher's where pennants fly like battle flags and the faces wait; pale faces waiting for disaster like children in a cinema waiting to be frightened. The Fossa, Valbus and Rutherfords are in the commentator's gabble, but Foinavon isn't far behind. Neither are Kirtle Lad, Bassnet, Different Class and Moidore's Token. The trouble with commentators is that they tend to watch one horse and one of the commentators is watching Different Class. Gregory Peck's horse gets more than his share and again we feel sorry for Foinavon.

The water jump is the sixteenth, and it's here, giving the stands a moment of horror, that Ronald's Boy comes down and stays down, bringing down Bassnet, Champion Prince and Foinavon. The 1967 winner is up at once, a leg through his reins. Unlucky but philosophical, making no attempt to chase the others in squandered effort, Foinavon looks for the paddock and lollops sensibly towards his lad.

Meanwhile the horse ambulance, drawn by black shires with white legs, creeps towards the water-jump. Ronald's Boy is still down, his head kept flat by jockey Harty. There is compassion in the pressure, but not only that; there is entreaty, too, begging the horse to lie still while veterinary assistants put the screens around.

At Becher's for the second time The Fossa is still in front, followed by Rondetto, Moidore's Token, Rutherfords and Different Class. We have to look back for Red Alligator, but the purple colours are coming. We need to look longer for Great Lark and when we cannot find him, we know why the hunting horns are silent and guess there'll be tears in the Liffey tonight.

Different Class is first over Valentine's, delighting the commentator whose public school enthusiasm has shaken a laugh from the stands. Red Alligator is next, then Rutherfords and Moidore's Token. They jump the twenty-eighth and begin the long gallop past the canal. Now it's all Red Alligator. Half the crowd seems to have come from Bishop Auckland or to have heard the whisper. Or perhaps they like to see a twenty-year-old riding like a veteran. Yesterday Brian Fletcher fell in a minor steeplechase; this morning the doctors passed him fit. Now he's riding into history and making it look easy.

It's no race from the last. Red Alligator and Fletcher survive that long run-in which destroyed First of the Dandies and Carrickbeg and so many others in the name-filled past. Moidore's Token is second, twenty lengths away. Different Class is a disappointed third. Rutherfords is fourth and Ronald's Boy is dead.

There is a special cheer for Tim Durant, sixteenth of the seventeen to finish, his thin face cracking a grin to the crowd, his 'V' sign to the bookmakers a promise to collect £500. He gives it to the Injured Jockeys' fund and makes do with champagne.

Suddenly it's over; the 127th Grand National and the 124th to be run at Aintree. It might have been the last because in the climate of doubt and rumour any Grand National might be the last. But it did not seem to be the last. There was no sense of mourning among the spectators, no cloud of doom over Aintree. Perhaps it was the sunshine, for sunshine can transform; perhaps it was the paint, red and green and smelling like a spring-clean. But there seemed to be an optimism, not apparent in previous years, a lift of the spirit as though Aintree had escaped its 'death-wish' and become restored. If this is so, tradition is safe, the sport is richer, and the ghosts can walk unharmed.

2180217R00034

Printed in Great Britain
by Amazon.co.uk, Ltd.,
Marston Gate.